MARY, QUITE CONTRARY

*a Second World War girlhood
and what happened next*

Mary Essinger

Mary, Quite Contrary
Published by The Conrad Press in the United Kingdom 2016

Tel: +44(0)1227 472 874
www.theconradpress.com
info@theconradpress.com

ISBN 978-1-78301-884-0

Typesetting by:
Charlotte Mouncey, www.bookstyle.co.uk

The book cover and The Conrad Press logo were designed by Maria Priestley.

Printed by Management Books 2000 Limited
36 Western Road
Oxford
OX1 4LG

By the same author
Wounded Bird of Paradise
How to be a Merry Widow (as Mary Rogers)

For Theodore

CONTENTS

PREFACE

I love my computer and Google and the miracle of email. As for the idea of having a personal phone you can carry in your handbag and use to call anybody else in the world, it would have seemed like something magical to me as a child of the 1930s, when only one person in our street had a telephone at all.

Cars were hardly ever seen on the street in my village. We had a wireless but I was twenty-two years old before there was a TV in my house; Mam and Dad, like so many people, rented one for the coronation in 1953. As for computers, they weren't introduced into schools and colleges until the 1980s.

Necessity being the mother of invention, the spur for much of this technology was the Second World War, the backdrop to my childhood in Glenfield, a small village near Leicester in the English Midlands.

Seventy years ago children could play anywhere their legs could carry them, roaming in gangs over fields, back lanes, railway lines and brooks. But many stayed within calling distance of home where they could hear their mothers standing in the street shouting, 'Gordon, Sheila, your dinner's ready!'

We called our mother 'Mam' and not 'Mum', because 'Mum' was not a good shouting word, try it.

Today's children do not have that sense of freedom and the same opportunities for adventure we had because streets belong to cars now and cars can kill. To find somewhere to run and play and hide, a child usually needs a car to take them there.

We had no washing-machine, no fridge and no bank account or savings. Groceries bought from Walker's corner shop in the week were paid for on Saturdays from Friday's wage packet.

There were no carpets on the floor in our house, only lino and rugs. For hot water we had to put the kettle on except for bath night on Fridays when Mam lit the kitchen copper and pumped hot water upstairs into the bathroom. When lights suddenly went out there was a hunt in the dark for a shilling to slot into the electric meter under the stairs. The only warm room in winter was the living room called 'The House.'

'Where's Gordon?' 'He's in The House.'

All the family used the same towel. I don't even remember us having toothbrushes. I do remember that after the school dentist had looked at our teeth she gave us a sweet. The school doctor weighed and measured us.

Mam and Dad, who smoked Woodbines, walked over to the pub on Saturday nights to sing with their friends and drink Indian Pale Ale. On Sundays they had a lie-in while we children enjoyed our weekly treat of a penny chocolate bar and a biscuit in bed.

We didn't think of ourselves as poor because everybody we knew lived like that. Poor people wore ragged clothes and, unlike us, had no indoor lavatory or bathroom.

Life today, with its foreign travel and opportunities, is wonderful and beautiful. Television shows us the world. We can communicate with anyone. Would the hatred, militant nationalism and racism that led to the war I grew up in have been possible if we'd been Facebook friends with people from round the world?

Medical care is excellent. As for our standards of living today, even during recessions most people live in a way we could only have dreamed of when I was a girl.

Technology changes but people don't. We have the same feelings and emotions. We still feel happy, sad, worried, ambitious and disappointed.

Here, in *Mary, Quite Contrary*, by trying to remember not only what happened when I was a girl but what it felt like, I've tried to recapture it.

Mary Essinger

Please note that some names have been changed.

Part One

A Second World War girlhood

I
MY FIRST MEMORY

Memory is picky. Why does the recollection of some episodes of life stay with us and others vanish?

My first memory is this:

Mam needed mother-of-pearl buttons and she was letting me go all the way to the sewing shop to buy them.

'Are you sure you know where it is?'

'I know.'

'Will you promise to look both ways when you cross over near Bent's grocery shop?'

'Promise.'

'You're to come straight back.'

Holding the money tight in my hand I set off along Station Road to the Square then turned left into Dominion Road.

It was so exciting to be going out by myself for the first time. I could walk there or run, or even stop and look at things. I was a big girl now, nearly five.

Outside the shop I took the buttons from the paper bag to look at them sewn on the card with its silver paper backing. There were twelve small pearl buttons, four in each row, glimmering in different colours when I tilted them to the sun. They were made from a fish called oyster.

It was a long way home and my legs were getting tired. Along Station Road I could see Mam waiting at the gate waving to me.

Proudly I handed over the buttons and the change.

She put them down then held my face in her two hands.

'I was with you all the time worrying about you and imagining how far you'd got. You're a clever little girl but I will not let you out of my sight again for a long time. I've been so worried.'

Grown ups were silly.

II
Infant School 1937-1939

Gordon Allen came to school sitting on a white pony led by a man named Mr Parker who wore a black hat. Gordon wore a white suit and had shiny gold hair like a prince in my story book. All the way down Station Road we children ran alongside them.

On the day of Gordon's sixth birthday Mr Parker left a huge box of toffees for our teacher, Mrs Taylor, to give to the whole class. Mrs Taylor was short and round and when she turned her head the grey bundle of hair at the back wobbled.

Taking the lid from the big square box she showed us the rows of wrapped toffee bars, some in blue paper, some in pink, all beautiful.

'Now children, sit in a circle. I'm going to hold up these cards one by one and whoever calls out the letter correctly gets a toffee bar.'

I knew all the letters and called out each one loud, 'H', 'C','M','B', but she took no notice of me so I shouted them even louder. Still she did not look at me and listened only to the boys at the back. I coughed. Then she laughed out loud:

'All right, Mary, I know you're there,' and I got my toffee bar. It lasted ages, smooth caramel taste and a claggy feeling between my teeth.

At four o'clock there was Mr Parker waiting outside with the pony to collect Gordon and the children who had been invited to his birthday party. Like Gordon, they were from the big houses on Groby Road and in their best clothes, frilly things. Once again we trailed home with them, all part of the excitement. When we came to my house and I started to run in Mr Parker asked me who we paid our rent to. When I told him Allens he said, 'Go and ask your mum if you can come to the party, we'll wait for you.'

Quickly she changed my dress, tied a blue matching ribbon in my hair and said, 'Don't forget to thank Mr Parker and call in the shop on the way and ask for a quarter of liquorice allsorts. Tell her to put it on the bill.'

In Walker's shop I had to wait while she scooped out a shovel full of sugar from a sack standing on the floor and poured it into a blue paper bag on the scales. Then it was my turn. Clutching the sweets I soon caught up because they all had to wait at the crossing while the train went past.

Liquorice allsorts are pretty. Stripy cubes, pink cartwheels with a black middle and blue circles with sugar seeds. There was plenty of time to taste the earthy liquorice on the long uphill drag that summer afternoon.

With so many other presents I don't think Gordon noticed there were only five sweets left in the bag when I handed them over.

'Mind the road,' was always the last instruction as we set off for school every morning, the boys treading on shiny slugs that left black slime on their boots.

Home again at dinner-time then back to school till four o'clock. Not much traffic used Station Road, the main street through the village, so the ones that did come were unexpected. Pet cats and dogs were often found dead by the roadside. We buried ours in the garden with a funeral and singing.

My new puppy, Pal, was a tubby white terrier with brown patches and when he wagged his tail it banged on our sideboard. He liked chasing cars and vans and one afternoon he followed me to school. His little white legs went whizzing round the playground chasing the children as they squealed with excitement. At going in time Miss Graham, the nature teacher at the school, told me to take him home. I had no lead for him. Round the corner of the Square, near the Nag's Head pub, a big van came and Pal ran after it. The back wheel went over the middle of his body. The van stopped. I watched, trembling in fear and fascination as the little fat puppy sat in the road looking at me and wagging his tail while a pool of blood began to spread round him. Slowly he sank into the bright red shimmering jelly till he could move no more.

With a piece of sacking the driver grabbed Pal by his back legs and slung him in the back of the van calling out in a kindly way, 'I'll bury him for you.' A lady put her arm round me and told me the man was a farmer. For weeks afterwards I would stand by the roadside for ages before crossing even if nothing was anywhere in sight and I didn't eat meat for a week.

Five children were killed on that road. Once, on my way to Walker's shop I spoke to Noreen, a girl about three years old, who was playing in the street. I told her she was wearing a dirty dress. When I came out of the shop a big lorry was outside. The driver was carrying Noreen wide in his arms; her mother was running alongside in her apron crying out, 'Oh, my baby! Oh my baby!'

Noreen was the youngest of a big family and had many grown-up brothers. I felt really awful because I'd been bossy to her. Perhaps me telling her she had a dirty dress was the last thing anyone said to her.

Word went round the village that any child could call in Noreen's house to see her. The coffin rested on two chairs in the front room which was full of the smell of primroses. Covering her body was a white satin dress and she looked more chubby than in life. On her cheek was a small bruise and in her hand a bunch of violets with their stalks wrapped in silver paper.

While the grown ups whispered in the next room I stared at the beautifully dressed child lying so still and not at all as if she was asleep.

'Did you touch her?' mother asked later.

'No,' I answered quickly, feeling guilty because I had stroked the cold hand.

'Well you should have touched her then you won't dream about her,' was the reply.

Home was a house on the main road through the village. Upstairs were three bedrooms and a bathroom with no taps. David, my older brother, slept with Gordon who was younger, and mine was the small back bedroom overlooking fields. Every night when Dad bent over to tuck me in he said, 'Pray to Jesus that Daddy finds a good job.'

Dad was over six feet tall and had once been a policeman. Every night he put his false teeth in a glass. The teeth were a present for his twenty-first birthday and he never ate raspberries because the seeds might get stuck in his teeth.

The toilet was downstairs and one evening when I was about five I came down to wee.

Mam and Dad were listening to the wireless and, at first, did not hear me cry out that I was stuck in the wooden seat. They pulled and pulled but could not get me free. It hurt and I was frightened and crying all the time thinking the seat might never come off. With a screwdriver Dad undid the seat and carried me into the living room still trapped in it. They gave me a lemon biscuit while they smeared butter all round my bottom till finally I became loose.

Near the floor of the pantry was a wide stone slab to keep food cold. One day mother caught sight of a dog called Rex Hughes grabbing the Sunday joint off the slab and running up the street with it. That was our meat for the week. Dad complained to Rex's owner at the bike shop but he said we should have kept the door shut. Dogs were known by their family's name, Rex Hughes, Rover Smart, Rex Tetley.

Ginger Bent was a ginger coloured horse and he pulled the small carriage that delivered groceries from Bent's shop. When Ginger did his business in the street people ran out and picked it up with a shovel to put on their tomatoes. One day, walking along the footpath after visiting my grandmother on Groby Road, I climbed down the fifty-two steps, crossed the railway line where boys squashed ha'pennies into pennies, then another climb up the steep bank into the field.

Ginger came running up to me. Oh dear, there was no time to reach the stile. I backed into a hedge. He came up close to my face. I was terrified. He was so big and I was alone and thought I would be killed. Framed by the blue sky he looked down at me. His huge black velvet nostrils were so close I could smell his warm horsey breath. Although there were no houses nearby I shouted, 'Help', softly at first in case I startled him into an attack, then louder, then louder still. Help did not come and the hedge scratched my back.

After what seemed hours Ginger moved away to nibble grass. Without taking my eyes off him, I sidled along the prickly hedge inch by inch till I reached the safety of the stile. Once across I turned to see Ginger still chewing and taking no notice of me. I wandered home puzzled at having escaped such a dreadful death.

Feeling frightened was horrible, a wobbly feeling in my tummy that would not go away. Upstairs on a double-decker bus going to Leicester I was frightened going over the bridge and thought it would tip over and fall in the river. Mam was very worried when I had a cold and made me stay in bed drinking lemonade. That was because she thought I might die. Even our own garden was spooky in the dark with the apple tree branches waving in the wind like fierce animals. Under my bed was another frightening place. Once, settling down to sleep the bed lifted up. I thought it was imagination at first but it rose up again. I was terrified. Then, from that mysterious place under the bed, the top of a head appeared and I held my breath as my younger brother came out. I was so angry and hit him hard with a slipper. Perhaps he had seen me undressing and that was even more frightening.

Mam's hair was dark and curly. Her eyes were blue. Two front teeth stuck out with a gap between. She sang really loud round the house.

One day when we were young
One wonderful morning in May
You told me you loved me
When we were young one day.

Another song was about Russia.

I will come and find you
Break the chains that bind you
When the flowers break through the snow
I will surely come again
My lovely Russian rose.

'She looks as if she's just going to do a week's washing.' That's what Mam said if she saw a badly-dressed woman. Every Monday Mam put on her oldest clothes to do the washing.

Using a saucepan, she ladled cold water from the kitchen tap into the copper boiler that was bricked into the kitchen wall. Under the copper was a small fireplace with a little iron swing door. From the living-room fire she fetched a pan of burning coals shouting, 'Out of my way. Out of my way,' before shovelling the hot coals into the fireplace and banging the door shut with her foot.

After sorting out the washing into whites and coloureds she rubbed the stains using a big bar of green Fairy soap with a baby running along. First into the copper went the whites. After pouring Rinso from a red and blue pocket, she stirred them with a rolling pin. When they were ready they went into the sink for rinsing in something called bluebag to make them look whiter. After this the coloured clothes took their turn in the copper.

Next came the outside mangling, when the rinsed garments were squeezed between two rubber rollers and the water drained into a bucket. Sometimes the mangle broke the buttons if they were not linen ones. On to the washing line to dry went all the clothes; sheets had to be folded double or they reached down to the garden. A strong wind made pyjamas dance. Afterwards when the dry cotton sheets were gathered up off the line I pressed my nose to them and they smelt lovely. When it rained everything was hung up on strings high in the living room to dry, the dangling wet sheets flapped in our faces while we ate dinner.

The midday meal on Mondays was cold meat left from Sunday with cold potatoes fried up followed by rice pudding. The pudding went in the oven first thing and stayed on low all morning. It was always thin and watery and didn't taste nice except for the burned skin round the edge of the dish, we children fought over that. Also on Mondays the table was covered with newspaper because the table-cloths were in the wash. We read the newspaper while we ate. Everything had to be ready for ironing by Wednesday.

The dobby hole was the dark, curtained-off area under the stairs where we played among old clothes and Wellingtons.

One Monday morning my younger brother dashed out of the dobby hole holding something by the tail.

'What's this?' he called to Mam who was hidden in clouds of steam and the soapy smell of boiling clothes.

'Oh, my goodness,' she shrieked, 'it's a dead rat. Take it outside. Wear this old glove, try not to touch it. I'll kill that cat, bringing vermin in.'

We lowered the dead rat into a bucket at the top of garden, using a wooden board for a lid.

'Now don't go anywhere near. Your dad can bury it when he gets home and for goodness sake shut that cat in the coal-house.'

Timmy, our tabby cat, was running round wailing looking for his rat. 'Look in the dobby hole to see if there's any mess,' she said, 'and keep the glove on; you can catch the plague from rats. I'll never be finished this morning.'

In the dobby hole was another dead rat so now we had two in the bucket and mother was still going on about it.

'Your dad can get on to the council. It's a downright disgrace.'

All morning we waited for our big brother, David, to come home; he was older and out with his friends playing with a chemistry set. He was too clever to play with us but that morning we had something important to tell him for a change.

'Guess what we've got in a bucket, two dead rats.'

'Show me,' he said, as if he didn't believe us.

'Just let David have a quick look, that's all,' mother called, sliding the wooden clothes prop along the line, 'then put the lid straight back before any germs can get out.'

We followed as he sauntered up the garden and lifted the lid. He bent over and peered inside before turning to us and saying as if we were babies, 'They're not rats. They're kittens. And they're not dead.'

'Go on?' Mam said, creeping forward with a clothes peg in her mouth. We gathered round, and there, in the bottom of the bucket, were two creatures with no eyes rolling over each other and squeaking.

David strolled back into the house calling over his shoulder, 'I told you that cat was female.'

'Oh, my godfathers,' mother groaned, 'that poor, poor, mother cat. Let him out of the coal-house this minute and carry those beautiful kittens back inside.'

By the time Dad came home we'd made a bed of old clothes in the dobby hole and put Timmy in with the four babies; there were two more under the coats. We gave the cat some rice pudding and squatted round to watch the babies tugging and pulling at the fur. Dad said they were sucking milk, but we couldn't see any.

David had his own bedroom and when we were all in bed I called to him, 'David'. No answer.

'David.'

'I'm reading.'

'What does "female" mean?'

We waited a long time for his answer.

'A mother cat. A she cat. They have kittens.'

Our David knew everything.

At school I wrote 'We had plumonj for tea.' Looking over my shoulder the teacher started to laugh but in a nice way. 'That's not how it's written.'

'Well, what is it then?' She hesitated at first as if she didn't know what to say then explained that it was a French word 'blancmange' that meant 'white eat'. I thought what a strange word and what a funny language.

25

On either side of the fireplace in the living room were two black iron ovens but for cooking we used the electric stove in the kitchen.

Our cat went missing one cold day. We could hear him meowing but could not find where the noise was coming from. We searched and searched. It was puzzling; the sound was coming from somewhere near the fireplace. Then Dad opened one of the ovens and out he jumped.

Clive Harris, a big man in brown cap, lived in West Street in our village and would drown unwanted kittens for tuppence; they floated on top of a water butt that smelt terrible. To kill a rabbit he charged one shilling. Dad said it was a waste of money and he could easily kill a rabbit himself. A man at work told him what to do; you stretched it out then hit it hard on the back of its neck. It was nearly Christmas and we were going to eat our pet rabbit called Alice after she'd been fattened up with dandelions and balls of warm mashed potato mixed with linseed oil that smelt really nice.

We were sent out to play while he did the killing. Later, we come back to find her hanging by the back legs on the white-washed brick wall of the kitchen with newspaper on the floor to catch drips of blood from her nose.

'Where's Dad?'

'Leave him alone,' Mam whispered, 'don't talk to him, he's in the front room, don't go in, he's very upset.'

In the morning he said, 'Next time I need to kill a rabbit I'll go to Clive Harris, it'll be worth every penny.'

On Christmas Day Mam said to David, 'Why aren't you eating your dinner?'

'I don't fancy it,' he said, 'I don't want to eat Alice.' After that I wouldn't eat any more and nor would our small brother.

In the Co-op on Stamford Street women were chatting while they watched the man slicing bacon on a machine. Maureen

Briggs who went to my school was there, she was a pale girl who walked smoothly without ever turning her head. Mrs Briggs, dressed all in grey, said, 'My Maureen plays the piano, she goes to the piano teacher every week.' All the mothers turned to look at Maureen and asked her about her lessons. Piano-playing seemed an important thing to do so I knocked on the door of the piano teacher to ask if I could come for lessons.

'Yes, of course you can. Ask your mother to come and see me.' She paused and added, 'You'll have to practise at home all the time.'

'Practise?'

'Yes. Is your piano in good tune?'

'We haven't got a piano.'

'Oh', she said, looking down at me from the top step of her doorway, 'it's no good having piano lessons if you have no piano.'

Next time I saw Maureen I said, 'I can play the piano.'

A few days later Mrs Briggs invited me to tea; Mam washed my hair the night before in camomile flowers to make it more yellow.

Mrs Briggs was not a nice lady and nobody spoke at tea-time.

After tea she said, 'Now Mary, did you tell Maureen you could play the piano?'

'Yes, I think I did.'

'Well, come into the front room and let's hear you play.'

She led me to the front room that smelt cold and damp, gave me a cushion to sit on and waited. I stared at the keys then leaned forward to peer at the music and said it was too small for me to see.

'That's all right, I'll bring you a larger print.'

I stared at that music as well, feeling silly. At last her mother spoke.

'You see, let that be a lesson to you Maureen, if people tell lies you can be sure they will be found out.'

It wasn't telling lies, it was pretending.

This is how we made a fire.

Old newspapers

A tied up bundle of firewood from the shop

Swan Vestas matches

Small pieces of coal

Some sugar.

First the fireplace had to be cleaned out from the night before and some newspaper scrunched up in it. Criss-crosses of about six sticks of wood were placed on top of the newspaper then a few pieces of coal about the size of a plum. Striking Swan Vestas matches till they burst into flames with a nice smell, Dad lit the paper that quickly curled, crackled and went brown at the edges, then the wood caught fire with a hiss.

After that a long wait till the coal caught a flame. If it didn't catch light properly Dad used a dustpan to support a whole sheet of newspaper in front of the fire to get it going, first throwing on a spoonful of sugar that made the flames behind go whoosh. Sometimes the big sheet of paper caught fire and Dad had to bundle it quickly into the fireplace with his hands.

Later, when the fire was burning without flames you could make good-tasting toast on it if it didn't fall off the toasting fork. In the hot embers you could roast a potato, peeling off the black skin when it was ready. Mam curled her hair by pushing the curling irons in the red coals till they were hot then she took them out and wiped the soot off before winding her hair between the two prongs. Sometimes the curling irons were too hot and her hair crackled and shrivelled up. To iron

28

clothes Mam placed one of a pair of flat irons on a stand in the fire, when it was hot she wiped any soot off before ironing the washing. By the time it had cooled down the other iron was ready.

Before going to bed we kept the fire going all night by throwing slack on it. Mam had burn marks on her leg from sitting too close to the fire. Lots of women in the village had them.

Chimneys had to be swept or the soot caught fire sending flames into the air and filling the street with smoke.

The chimney-sweep came in summer. Black bike, black poles tied on, black face, black cap and black round brush. Mother covered the furniture with old sheets.

First the sweep laid some sacking to catch the soot then fixed a big black cloth to cover the fireplace. Then, lifting it up like a skirt, he went to work underneath, pushing in a pole with the brush on then adding more poles as he poked it up the chimney. Everywhere smelt of soot. We waited till he told us, then our job was to run outside and shout as soon as we saw the brush coming out of the chimney top. Afterwards the soot was spread on the back garden to help the cabbages grow.

Nothing much grew in our garden only rows of cabbages, flowers called Night-Scented Stock and an apple tree with no apples. If we were short of anything Mam sent us across the road, saying something like, 'Ask Mr Williams for a penny worth of parsley.'

A small gate in the back garden fence opened on to a farmer's field where my brothers played French cricket with a crippled boy next door and where, with bare feet, I once trod on a bee and hopped round screaming.

Looking through my bedroom window one dark morning I saw some strange shapes outside.

'Mam, Dad, there's cows in the garden.' There they were, seven black cows like huge statues sitting chewing. All the cabbages had disappeared. The gate must have been left open. Dad ran downstairs pulling a coat over his pyjamas. He poked a cow with a rake but it took no notice and looked the other way. Even Mam who was frightened of cows lifted up the line prop and banged a cow on its bottom but it carried on chewing. They did not want to move. We children shouted at them. Gradually, one of them slowly lumbered itself up and the others followed. It took ages to squeeze them through the little gate and Dad was late for work. Mam was crying, there was nothing left growing in the garden even the grass was flat and covered in cow muck and the smell was like a farmyard.

At the top of the field was a pond and one summer evening frogs were all round the edge on each other's backs making a lot of noise. Dad said, 'When the frogs are too old the young ones climb on their backs and strangle them.' We believed him.

David got scarlet fever and had to go to Groby Road Isolation Hospital. A man came to our house and burnt yellow sulphur to fumigate all the rooms to stop us catching it. I watched him doing it. 'Fumigate' seemed a very funny word.

In hospital when he'd eaten his boiled egg David turned the empty shell upside down in the egg cup. The nurse said, 'Didn't you want your egg David?' That was a good trick.

On the sands at Skegness, where my family went with Mam's sister-in-law Auntie Ada, Mam won a prize in a treasure hunt – a bottle of talcum powder - a beautiful bottle of thick green glass with white swirls behind. The top was gold and when it slid back it showed the holes and the smell was lovely and powdery. She let me hold it. I was 9 years old.

We children loved Auntie Ada, who had dark hair like a gypsy, because she said rude words which we dare not say; words like 'tits' and 'bum.' She came running along the sand with ice-cream cones and told us the war had started and perhaps we'd all better pack our suit cases and go home.

Lots of people were at the station but we managed to get a compartment to ourselves; Auntie Ada saved it for us while we all went to the WC because there were no corridors and no stops till Leicester. You had to keep the window closed till the train started or the carriage would be full of steam and sooty smells and noise. A big leather strap held the window down. On the wall was a picture of seaside place called Frinton and a sign saying, 'Please keep your feet off the seats.'

In the village one morning every iron gate and fence was ripped up by gangs of workmen to make munitions for our brave boys. Except for big houses, they didn't have their gates taken away. There was lots of excitement when a convoy came through and we waved at the soldiers sitting on the massive tanks, each with a King George's flag on the side. It seemed to take all morning.

While we stood eating our sandwiches we watched Mr Hood next door help Dad dig a trench in the field by the hedge, digging and digging all the time. The trench was in case we were bombed out and had nowhere to live.

One Sunday dinner time a tiny plane was high in the sky – everybody came on the street to watch it.

'Is it one of ours?'

'No, it's Jerry all right.' Our planes went zoom zoom, German planes just went zoom. From somewhere came a fighter plane chasing it and the small one broke up with black smoke bursting out. Everybody cheered and went back in to eat roast beef.

Next day Dad told us the two German airmen waited by a gate in Anstey till the Home Guard came to fetch them.

Copper Dyson, the policeman's wife, made a dress from one of the parachutes.

Some houses did not have an indoor lavatory; it was outside and for a seat there was just a board with hole in over a huge metal bin. Once a week these full bins had to be collected and tipped into an open tank on the back of a lorry. We all held our noses as the terrible smell filled the street. During the war I was surprised to see women carrying the bins hoisted up on their shoulders, wearing brown boiler suits; the first women I'd seen in trousers. One of them stared at me with a horrible glare from her haggard face as if she hated me.

Even the gypsy woman who came round cleaning the drains with her bare hands full of gold rings; even she had a nice face and smiled at me.

Air-raid practice was good fun at school. One class at a time trailed out to the shelter in the playground. No talking, no running, go to your place and sit still. Inside just long bare, grey, rough concrete benches and a nice smell of wet cement, a clean and new sort of smell. The door had to be open all the time because it was hot inside.

On the front of the Sunday paper was a picture of our village showing a whole family named Esposito leaving with their suitcases. We knew all the children but we didn't know they were Italian; it didn't seem right but Dad said the father should have changed his nationality.

'Why do they have to leave?' I asked.

'Well we don't know whose side they're on,' said Dad.

Me:	'Whose side is Swithland on?'
Mam:	'If you mean Switzerland it's neutral.'
Me:	'What's neutral?'
Mam:	'They are on nobody's side they don't have wars.'
Me:	'Why can't we be neutral?'

Mam: 'Switzerland has too many mountains for fighting.'

Sometimes we went to a village called Swithland for a picnic in the woods. I mixed up the name with Switzerland. I mixed up a lot of things. I mixed up my grandma with the Queen.

At night not one light had to show in case German bombers could see where houses were. Blackout curtains had to be used. The ARP in uniforms and peak hats came round to all the windows, even the ones at the back and if there was a chink of light they knocked on the door and called, 'There's a light showing.' No street lights were on and any car lights had to be dimmed with black tape. You could wear a luminous button on your lapel, it glowed in the dark. All windows had to have brown sticky tape stuck on like an X-shape to stop them shattering if there was a hit.

Dad was sometimes called out to help people. A woman knocked on the door once to fetch him because her mother was fat and could not get out of the bath. At their house when Dad was going upstairs the daughter shouted:

'All right mum, here's a man coming to help.'

'Oh dear,' shouted the mother, 'is he married?'

I couldn't stop thinking about the lady in the bath with no clothes on. Perhaps she put a towel round; it wouldn't have mattered if it got wet.

Old Mr Eaton was not a friendly man; he looked a bit like Hitler when he stared at us. When Mr Eaton was dying Mrs Eaton knocked on our door to ask Dad to help her. Dad was gone a long time and when he came back he told us that before Mr Eaton died he grabbed his wife by the throat. 'I pulled him off.' Dad said, 'I would have broken his arm if I'd had to.'

Dad wanted the boys to grow up tough so he taught them how to box: 'Come on, come on, hit me.'

Sometimes Dad woke the boys in the middle of the night to listen to the American boxing on the wireless. I came down as well because I didn't want to miss anything. We all huddled close to hear it better. 'And a left, and a right, and another left, he's down, no he's up again…'

Dad pointed at the front and said to me, 'One day there'll be pictures on this as well as sound, you'll be able to see people.' That was silly because the screen was so small and covered in names like Luxembourg and Helvetia. He said the sound came through the air in pockets and I imagined pockets like those in my dress.

Old Mr Foster in the village mended clocks. He walked folded over with a stick. When I went to collect our clock he showed me something called a crystal set made with real cats guts. 'Put your ear close,' he said, 'What can you hear?'

'A lady singing but she's a long way away.' He said there would be no charge for the clock because all he'd done was leave it in the oven all night. 'Mostly they just want warming up,' he said.

In winter the insides of the window in my bedroom were frosted over and I couldn't understand how the frost got inside through the glass.

The pattern was beautiful, like swirls of leaves, as if somebody had drawn them. To see through the window I had to scrape a hole with my fingernail.

In the village hall, we tried gas masks on to find the right size. I had to pull mine over the front of my head, the rubber smelled awful and I could hardly see through the celluloid eye shield and I couldn't hear and I hated it.

Every day we had to carry our gas mask to school in a square brown cardboard box with strings dangling. You were sent home if you forgot it.

And we still had to watch the roads. Dashing across without looking I once ran into the path of a car, feeling the whoosh of air as it just missed me. I reached the safety of the far pavement, trembling with fear and then bewilderment as water trickled down my leg to form a puddle on the ground. Further along the road the car had stopped; perhaps the driver had been scared too, then he drove off. I knew the driver but at that time he did not know me because I was still at the infants' school and he was the man they called Gaffer, headmaster of the juniors.

III
JUNIOR SCHOOL 1939-1942

'Top' school on Kirby Lane, with lavatories across the yard instead of inside, was the next stage up from the infants and we all worried about Gaffer, the tough headmaster. His name was Mr Perrin and he was the only male teacher left; all the others had gone to war.

Short and stocky with big yellow teeth, he wore corduroy trousers and a green tweed jacket that went with his curly ginger hair. Inside the school knotted wooden floorboards bounced and creaked under our feet and everywhere smelt of chalk. The three classrooms were heated by shovelling coke into a round iron stove and when you spat on the top the ball of spit danced across ending in a tiny explosion.

School mornings began with Gaffer banging out hymns on the piano. All the doors were open and although we could not see children in other classrooms we could hear them.

Ye Holy Angels Bright
Immortal Invisible God Only Wise

A favourite was *Praise to the Holiest in the Height;* because when we came to 'And in the garden secretly,' Gaffer played softly and we had to sing it in a whisper, sometimes so quiet we could hear the cows coming back from milking.

Oh Valiant Hearts was about soldiers dying and made me cry. Sheila Davy cried as well but I could make more tears.

Days ended as they began with Gaffer at the piano this time leading the singing of

Now the day is over, night is drawing nigh
Shadows of the evening fall across the sky.

Then the long walk back home along Station Road to Mam's usual enquiry, 'What did you do at school this afternoon?'

Pretending to be thinking about something else I muttered, 'Nothing.'

One winter morning, having put on scarves and gloves the boys went early to school to make a slide on the steep slope of the playground. Queuing up they took turns in thick grey shorts, falling socks and black boots to make a run at it before sliding down sideways with arms out. Soon the ice was all green and glassy.

Somebody shouted, 'Here's Gaffer,' and everybody waited to see what he would do.

'Stand back,' he ordered, 'all of you stand back.' He pulled off his scarf, took a run at the slide and, crouching down with arms wide, went whizzing down to the bottom. Everybody clapped.

'Right, just five minutes more and then you boys cover this ice with ashes from the coke shed. Ice is dangerous we don't want the girls falling on it.'

The cry of, 'Gaffer's coming' was the signal to stop whatever we were doing. On the way home two dogs were mating and we formed a giggling circle round them, aware that we were doing something vaguely wrong.

'Gaffer's coming.' He stopped the car and came to see what was happening.

Without a word he joined the circle, waited till it was over and drove away.

Gaffer smoked as he taught, knocking the bowl of his pipe on the heavy table. With chalk in one hand and the other wrapped round the blackboard, step by step, he explained the mystery of fractions by drawing a circle on the board. 'Now if this is a cake I can divide it into two exact halves. Then I can cut it into quarters. Now if you add one half to one quarter how much have you got? Yes, Mary.'

'Three quarters, sir.'

'Good. How do you write that down?'

'Three over four, sir.'

'Right. Now all of you take these fractions down.'

Dipping pens in the watery ink (pencils were for babies) we copied down the funny signs for quarters, halves and three quarters while Gaffer filled his pipe. The ink wasn't poisonous even if it smelt funny because Kenny Blunt drank some once and he didn't die.

Girls liked Gaffer's class but the boys were afraid of him.

The warmest place in the schoolyard was the outside wall of the boiler room where bricks were worn smooth. One winter morning Ann, a pale girl with a limp, had been pushed away from her place at the wall and the boy that did it got reported by one of Gaffer's elected prefects. He called the boy to the front and shouted at him,

'What, you pushed Ann away! You bully, you selfish bully! That girl's a cripple,' and he flung the boy against the bookshelves then whacked his leg with a cane.

Later, the prefect told me she would not have reported the boy if she'd known Gaffer would hit him.

'We need a new cane,' he said one morning, flexing it over his knee. 'This one's getting weak. See if anybody can find me one. Anything strong, a bit of willow will do.'

We looked round at each in other. Was this a joke? What child would bring a cane for a teacher? But one child did. Audrey, the creepy goody-goody of the class with two neat long plaits, the sneak, the one we never played with. She brought a willow stick to school the next day and hid it under the bench.

'Now, did anybody bring me a new cane?' he enquired with a smile. We did not know whether he was making fun of us or not. Audrey stood up, waving the stick.

'I've brought you one, sir.'

'Thank you Audrey.'

As she returned to her desk he swished the new cane in the air.

'Now let me see if it works, this new implement. Who shall we practise on first?'

This must be one of his jokes; surely he wouldn't just pick a child to try it on.

'Audrey, come here dear, let's see if your very nice present is any good.'

She looked round.

'Come on Audrey we haven't got all day. Put your hand out,' and he swiped her with the new cane.

Gaffer was producing one of the short play scenes he did with us and a boy named Keith was supposed to say, 'My dear Oliver,' only it kept coming out as 'My dear Holiver' with an 'H'. Over and over again Gaffer tried to make him say 'Oliver' but he couldn't. Each time Keith spoke he pronounced it as 'Holiver'.

'My dear OLIVER', Gaffer shouted. 'OLIVER, now say it!'

This time it was Keith who lost his temper. Red in the face he yelled:

'I can't do it and I ain't goin' try!'

Everything went quiet. Through the thin walls the whole school must have heard Keith shouting. No one had ever dared to answer Gaffer back. We waited. Gaffer grabbed Keith, shook him by the shoulders, threw him to the floor and hit his legs with the cane saying, 'You what! You speak to me like that?'

Stunned and frightened we stared down at our desks. Keith lay in a heap crying. It wasn't fair, he just could not say the word without the H sound, and he'd tried hard.

When school had finished, Gaffer kept Keith behind and we waited at the gate till he came out.

'What happened?'

'Nothing.'

'Go on. Tell us. Did he hit you again?'

Keith kicked at the dry cowpats in the narrow lane. At last he spoke.

'He said he was sorry.'

'You liar.'

'Yes he did. He said he was very sorry. And when we do the play I can say, "my dear young man" instead.'

Mr Everard of Everard's Brewery lived in the village and he came to our school to tell us about a poem called *We are Seven* by William Wordsworth which was in our poetry books.

I met a little cottage girl
She was eight years old she said
Her hair was thick with many a curl
That clustered round her head.
'Sisters and brothers little maid
How many may you be?'
'How many? Seven in all,' she said
And wondering looked at me.

The girl in the poem explained that she had six brothers and sisters, two brothers were at sea, two lived in a place called Conway and a sister and brother were in the churchyard.

'But they are dead, those two are dead
Their spirits are in heaven.'

'twas throwing words away for still
The little maid would have her will and said
'Nay master, we are seven.'

The girl in the poem lived in a cottage by the churchyard and in summer took a little porringer and ate her supper there. I wasn't sure what a porringer was; I thought it must have been an old-fashioned word for a porridge bowl.

Mr Everard said the poem showed that the girl was a true believer who knew that children went to heaven when they died. Then he held up a sixpence piece and said, 'I'll be back on Friday and I will give this sixpence to any child who has learned the poem by heart.'

Sixpence. Just for learning a poem by heart! I knew a lot of poems by heart and this one was easy to learn, seven verses and once I knew the first line of each verse the rest just came. It took a long time for Friday to come and my chance to recite it in front of the whole school and collect the money.

This wasn't the only school competition. Miss Ellis, the nature teacher, made a chart on the wall with pictures of wild flowers down one side. The first child to bring in one of the flowers had their name written next to it, and the one with most names would win a prize.

In summer evenings I scoured the fields and hedges with Eileen. Eileen was not clever at school and she had a stammer but she was brave and tall with ginger hair, scared of nothing and did anything I told her to do. Eileen said her Mam liked her to play with me because I was refined.

'What does refined mean?' I asked my mother. She thought about it for a while then said it meant I was not common.

Opposite the Railway Inn we found Cuckoo Pint and Field Bindweed and up the bank a yellow flower with the funny name of Cinquefoil. Meadow Sweet, with its summer smell, grew beside the brook and I almost trod on the tiny Scarlet Pimpernel.

One flower in the cornfield left a smell of pineapple on my fingers. Eileen and I were neck and neck on the competition list and way ahead of all the others.

One evening we searched along the railway line towards Ratby, the furthest we'd ever been, looking for a flower called Purple-Tufted Vetch. Jumping from sleeper to sleeper was easy at first but if we went too fast we tripped because some sleepers were closer together than others and made us lose our footing.

Leaving the train line we wandered through a field of sheep then over a ditch to another field. A fenced-off area by a ditch said, 'Sewage Works, Keep Out.' Over the fence small tomatoes were growing in straight lines row on row. We could pick some to take home. I climbed over first and as soon as my foot touched the ground it sank in; then the other foot slid into the soft smelly soil. I was terrified. I grabbed the fence, Eileen held my hand tight while I struggled to pull my foot out; my sandal was nearly sucked away.

Somehow I managed to get back over and wiped the soil off my leg with a handful of long grass. Hopping to the bank of the ditch where it was just deep enough to sit and dangle my feet in the chilly water I saw it. Next to where we were sitting was a bush of Purple-Tufted Vetch. One of the rarest flowers on the list and we had found it. The flower head was small nodding its head like a miniature sweet pea and along its stem were tiny pea pods full of seeds and little tendrils that clung to everything. The stalks were tough and hurt our hands when we tried to pull them free but we soon had enough to carry an armful home.

But who would be the first to get to school and have their name on the list and win the prize?

'I'm getting up really, really early with my dad. I'll be there first,' Eileen called with her excited stammer as she ran home waving her bunch.

Next morning I watched at the gate waiting for Miss Ellis to pass by on her way to school. Matching my step to hers I strolled along with her; she was a big lady and walked slowly.

'Miss, look what I found last night.'

'Oh, that's Purple-Tufted Vetch,' she said, 'I wondered if that would turn up. I'll put your name down as soon as we get to school.'

'When does the competition end?' I asked, knowing it was that very day.

'Twelve o'clock, then I'll give out the prize.'

At the school gate Eileen was waiting to thrust her bunch at Miss Ellis.

'You're just too late, Eileen. I'm sorry but that flower has already been found.' The prize was a book called *Out with Romany by the Sea* about puffins.

I won the prize. Eileen didn't seem to mind.

Uncle Syd, Uncle Ron and Uncle Jack went to the war. Mam went door-to-door asking people to sell her their clothing coupons because Auntie Lily was getting married and needed forty yards of stuff called scarlet taffeta and I was going to be a bridesmaid. I had to go for a fitting to a lady in Tudor Road who made the dresses for me and five other bridesmaids. Auntie Lily, who was always buying new things like gramophone records, was eighteen and getting married because Uncle Allen was going to be an airman and wear his uniform for the wedding.

My dress had long sleeves coming to a point on my hand. The neck was heart-shaped with rows of tiny buttons and loops all made from the taffeta stuff. It felt stiff and made a swooshy noise when I walked round the room in it. The night before the wedding Mam tore strips from an old sheet and twisted them round my hair to make curls. They felt lumpy on my pillow. The other bridesmaid had short straight hair but she looked nicer than me. She was pretty.

Instead of a dangling bouquet Auntie Lily carried five stalks of big white lilies. At the wedding Auntie Ada whispered to her, 'Come off it Lily, you're not that pure.' Auntie Lily was cross about it.

We were not allowed to call our grandmother anything except 'Mamma' because the word grandma would make her feel old, she said.

She ran Anstey Grange Guest House on Groby Road, wore dresses specially made, and was never to be argued with. The entrance to the huge stone house was by a drive round the lawn. I loved the low bay windows at the front where I could sit on the sill of the open window with my feet touching the ground outside.

The walls of the main entrance hall were made of wood and the wide, wide stairs curved round. When nobody was looking I walked slowly up and down the green carpet held in place with brass rods. The treads were so shallow I didn't even have to hold the banister. I felt like a grown up lady.

Sometimes I helped in the kitchen reaching over the massive serving table used for everything, rolling pastry, preparing meals and dishing out the food (bigger portions for the men). Mamma did the cooking on the long black cooking range. Albert was a waiter and people made fun of him because he wore a white waistcoat and a bracelet and smelt nice. His black hair was slicked back and he spoke in a squeaky voice. Instead of walking he seemed to glide.

I wasn't allowed to serve in the dining room because there were important people there, sometimes men to do with the war. One of the men showed me a round red tin with a string dangling from it. 'Pull the string,' he said, and when I did a crackly voice said, 'Crikey! That's Shell that was!'

After dinner I helped Albert put all the crockery back onto the shelves of the Welsh dresser that ran along the furthest wall of the second kitchen. Plates had to stand up; big ones on the top shelf, then side plates lower down and tiny coffee cups in a row on the bottom.

There was a small room called the butler's pantry where silver was polished and another called the still room full of glasses and bottles.

I spent all day helping in the kitchen once and Mamma gave me one pound and ten shillings, the most money I'd ever had. I went straight to town on the bus and bought an inkwell from the Midland Educational in Market Street; a heavy grey marble one, square but with curved corners and a well in the middle. It was really beautiful and I had bought it with my own money. When I showed it to Mam she was really cross and said I should have given her the money not wasted it.

Grandpa once gave me a ride in his green car to Ratby and we ran over a hen. 'Look, look grandpa, it's run out at the back, it's all right."

He didn't answer, he didn't speak much and he looked worried most of the time.

Uncle Ron worked for Freers and Blacks on the bread round before he was called up and he wrote to my mother every week on something called an airgraph. It was like a photo of a letter with tiny writing all on one small page. Some things were crossed out by the censor. The new man on the bread round who had not been called up came in for a cup of tea and my mother read Ron's letter to him. Afterwards the man told all the people on the round what was in the letter. 'He's in the Chindits now in the desert and has to drive Winston Churchill round.'

Auntie Jesse, Uncle Ron's wife, had used up all her coal allowance and after tea at her house we sat round the fireplace. Auntie Jesse said it was a funny thing to sit looking at an empty fire grate but it felt warmer. Dad said it was psychological. Now I knew what that word meant.

Mam and Dad had been to one of the big parties that Mamma gave in the main lounge at the Grange and next morning she told us there was a fat man there named Mr Wickwar and he made people laugh all the time. They played a game where you had to take some clothes off if you missed a turn.

Mr Wickwar took his trousers off and underneath he was wearing his wife's long-legged pink silk knickers. Everybody screamed with laughter and Mrs Wickwar shouted, 'So that's where they'd gone!'

Mrs Wickwar sent for Mam once and when she got there Mrs Wickwar was waiting in the kitchen crying. 'What can I do with him, Daisy, he's been in his chair for hours. He's been working at Coventry all night helping to pull people out of the bombed houses. He keeps saying it was the children, the little children. Little children dead. That's why he's crying. I can't do anything with him.'

So that Mam and Dad could stay late we three children were all sleeping overnight in one bed at Mamma's listening to the music and laughter of a big New Year party downstairs, grown ups only.

During the night Mam and Dad woke us up; we had to get dressed in our warm clothes half asleep, and trudge all the way home in the snow and the dark. Mam was very cross and grumbling all the time. There had been an argument with Auntie Lily. "Fancy making my children get out of a warm bed just because she wanted it for two of her posh friends, selfish little madam."

Mamma paid for us to go to the Christmas pantomime at the Opera House and when we settled in the best seats I looked round for her. She wasn't there, she hadn't come in. I wished she'd come in with us.

But the show was wonderful. First the orchestra played with a lovely tinny sound then the lights went out and the curtains opened. Oh, what a magical scene, the brightness and the colour. Blue birds were flying in the sky and a girl was sitting on a balcony watering red plants. She had dark hair and a striped pinafore. The other side of the stage was a baker's shop with cakes and loaves and a man wearing a blue striped apron and a straw boater. It looked real but it wasn't real, it was all painted on. Just painted.

The pantomime was *Cinderella* but they kept interrupting the story with somebody singing, then some girls doing ballet, then two comics telling jokes and it had nothing to do with the story at all but they were funny and made us laugh out loud. One threw a bucket of water over us and we all screamed but instead of water, bits of silver paper floated down. The Ugly Sisters were really men, you could tell, they wore ginger wigs and padded busts and were so fat in bundles of clothes they had to waddle across the stage, where they lifted up their skirts and showed long legged knickers. One had a purple dress with big yellow spots, the other wore pink with purple spots.

The prince in the story was really a lady, she hadn't even tried to look like a man, she had long hair, tied back. It was silly.

The comics came on again, and unrolled a chart with the words of a song, at first upside down. Everybody had to shout, 'It's the wrong way up.' At first they pretended they didn't hear us and we shouted louder. Then they pretended they didn't understand what we meant. One of them pointed to the words with a stick and there was a competition to see which side of the room could sing loudest. We had to do it twice.

At the end a real white Shetland pony was led across the stage pulling a silver coach with Cinderella, who was now a princess, wearing a sparkling silver dress. It was so lovely and everybody clapped and clapped.

I wanted to go on the stage when I grew up, not to be a princess because I wasn't pretty, but I could do acting. All you had to do was say words and that was easy. Of course you'd have to remember them as well.

Although I had never been to see a proper play at a theatre I wrote to the manager of Leicester's Theatre Royal asking if I could act in a play.

A letter came back from a man named Ronald Strong inviting me to see him. The last sentence said, 'Your parent or guardian will be welcome,' and Mam said it meant I should not go alone. She got all dressed up with lipstick and a perfume called Mischief.

We were shown into a room with easy chairs. First he made us a cup of tea then said there were plays on the wireless for girls reading boys' parts because girls' voices sounded like young boys. For the stage, juveniles had to start by changing scenery and helping actors. He asked me questions about English classes at school and while I was thinking about what to say Mam kept answering for me. I couldn't talk with her there, I just couldn't. Then he gave me something to read aloud and after that we left.

Outside in the street Mam was really cross, 'Why didn't you say something? Haven't you got a tongue in your head?' She told Dad about it saying how foolish she felt and I had no personality at all.

Pauline Smith lived down a yard that smelt funny where people shouted at each other all the time. She couldn't speak properly because her nose was full of snot and she wiped it on her shabby sleeve. I was sorry for her and decided to be kind and give her my bridesmaid's dress. Mam said it was all right because it was too small for me now even for playing at dressing up.

First I decided to tell Pauline about the dress and then give it to her later.

I waited till she came off the swing in the park and said,

'I'm going to give you my bridesmaid's dress.'

She ran off calling, 'Don't want it, I've got pwenty.'

Any spies coming would not know where they were because all the signposts came down and any shop with the village name had to have it painted over with dark brown paint. If anybody asked us children the way we had to say, 'I don't know,' even if we did, because careless talk costs lives.

Everybody had a ration book for food, even me, and we all had identity numbers; mine was RGJP 221/4, my small brother was RGJP 221/5 and we were supposed to remember them. The colour of the ration book was buff with tiny coloured threads in the paper. Babies had green ration books and they were sometimes allowed one orange. Mam said we were better off when rationing came in because food became cheaper. There was big excitement when Auntie Drucie in Canada sent a food parcel. *Aunt Jemima's pancake mix,'* it said on the box with a picture of a big smiling black lady in a check apron. We soon learned to mix the yellow powder with water and pour lots of round puddles into the pan, then you had to turn it over till it went a bit brown. It tasted lovely.

The Minister of Food gave recipes on the wireless; one was for mock crab made from carrots and potatoes. Sweets were rationed but there was not much money to spare for sweets anyway. I loved sweets and could never get enough.

I'd do anything for sweets, even bad things.

50

Alison Hargreaves, who lived in a big house, came out of the post office one morning holding a white paper bag with the top corners twisted. The only thing wrapped that way was sweets.

'What's in the bag?'

'Something for my grandfather, he has a sore throat.'

'Show me.'

She opened the bag. Blackcurrant lozenges coated in sugar, individually wrapped, and, because they were off ration, very expensive.

'Give me one.'

'I'm sorry, I can't do that.'

'Why not?'

'I promised grandfather I wouldn't eat one.'

Imagine that. Promising somebody that you wouldn't do something and KEEPING the promise even if they could not see you.

'He won't know how many there were. Give me one.'

'No.'

I snatched her stupid hat from her stupid head and said,

'If you don't give me one I'll throw your hat over this wall.'

The wall was high, the hat matched her coat and she looked worried.

'Well, come on. Do I get one or not?'

'My grandfather will be cross. I said I'd take them straight home.'

I raised my arm to throw the hat.

'All right, I'll explain to my grandfather that a girl said she would throw my hat over a wall if I did not give her one. Now please pass me my hat and I will give you a sweet.'

That blackcurrant lozenge tasted good but I felt bad about what I'd done. I wished I had clothes like Alison's and spoke nicely.

Lots of instructions came on the wireless from the radio doctor. We must all keep cheerful and healthy. The papers said he was going to talk about constipation and everybody listened in.

'You should go to the lavatory after breakfast and sit there till you have finished.' We talked about it all day at school because that was the rudest thing we'd ever heard on the wireless.

Mam: *The Americans are coming in now*
Me: *Whose side are they on?*
Mam: *Ours. We'll win the war now*

King George needed children to help him win the war. He wanted our ship ha'pennies to pay for guns. We also had to collect acorns and bring them to school in baskets for feeding pigs and collect rosehips from dog rose bushes to make syrup for babies.

Rosehips had bits of sticky white fur growing round the berry and it was while collecting them that we came across the mushroom field over the railway line, lots of them growing in rings in the green grass like golf balls of different sizes.

I curled my fingers over the smooth velvet tops, gave a twist and out they came with bits of soil stuck to the bottom of the stubby stalks. Underneath were delicate folds of pink with a lovely smell. My friend Mavis held out her dress while I placed them in gently so they didn't break. We had to find a few old mushrooms as well because Mavis said her Dad only liked them with maggots in.

Collecting waste paper and magazines door to door was another task for our class because waste paper could be pulped into ration books to help win the war. Mam said the only people having magazines would live in the big houses so that's where we went.

'Come tomorrow and I'll have them ready for you,' said a lady in Anstey Lane and we had a job the next day carrying home the boxes full of books.

Some of them were new. It was exciting; the whole family helped to sort them out. Imagine giving away new books. And not only books; there were embroidery patterns as well made of tissue paper with pictures of crinoline ladies watering flowers. We turned the paper upside down on a piece of cloth, pressed the back of it with a hot iron and the design came off on the cloth.

Also in the box was the heaviest book I'd ever held, *The Collected works of William Wordsworth* and it was beautiful. Much nicer than my school poetry book. The cover was made of dark green leather with gold writing on the front. The edges were bound with a sort of leather braid. Inside the front and back covers were stiff purple pages in a dark swirling pattern like marble and the hundreds of poems were printed on fine crinkly paper in small letters. Dad said I could keep it because it was wrong to send it for pulping but I had to hide it because there were a lot of blank spaces in it and my brothers used blank spaces in any book for drawing on.

Anstey Lane was also a good place to go carol singing but we started a week too early. 'Come at Christmas,' people shouted from inside after we'd sung carols with all the words right, so the boys finished with, *Wild Shepherds washed their socks by night* and *Oh come let's kick the door in.*

But Christmas Eve was another matter; nearly every house gave us money on Christmas Eve. There were six of us, my two brothers, Eileen with her brother and Kenny, a boy who hardly spoke but followed us everywhere we went and copied everything we did.

I was afraid of the long spooky drives up to the front door.

We'd just started singing outside one house when the door opened and a lady with ginger hair said, 'Come inside all of you, shake the snow off and wipe your feet on this mat.' When the lady went to close the door she called to Kenny who was standing back in the dark. We knew he wouldn't come in.

'Come inside out of the cold,' she ordered and in he came with his eyes down. We all shuffled into a hall with walls made of wood and a Christmas tree with candles lit up and a fairy with wings on the top.

'Stand round here and wait for me,' she said arranging us round the fire and she came back pushing an old man in a wheelchair; he was wearing a suit and tie with a check blanket over his knees. She asked which carols we knew and when we said, "all of them," she told us to start with *Hark the Herald*. As soon as we'd finished one carol I started us singing another straight away because it was warm inside and I wanted to stay a long time.

All the while we were singing she kept glancing at the man and smiling at him while he stroked his knees with long thin yellow fingers. Afterwards she brought in mince pies on a silver tray and cocoa, wished us a Merry Christmas and gave me an envelope which I thought was a card.

Such excitement when we all sorted everything out in the light of our house. There were four one pound notes in the envelope. With the money from other houses to spread on the table and count, it came to nearly six pounds, nine shillings and sixpence. I gave two shillings to Kenny who was waiting by the back door and told him to go home. Then we divided it up between us. And for once my Dad didn't ask us for any.

Evangelina, Eva for short, wore a white dress with a pink sash. She was kind to slaves stroking their chains with her dainty fingers as she walked among them holding the hand of her tall handsome father in his top hat looking down at Uncle Tom at the slave market.

Uncle Tom's Cabin, a green book with a raised pattern all round was a Christmas present. Inside the front cover it says, 'To Mary, best wishes from Mamma and Grandpa, Xmas 1941.'

Only it was Dad who wrote it in the book, I knew his hand writing.

Boxing Day. Dad took us along the footpath to Groby (you said 'Grew-bee') through icy fields and a great silence of snow. I wore my pixie hood and breathed out smoke. Jumping on long grass we shook white powder everywhere. Sunshine made diamonds in the drifts.

Groby Pool was a lake near Groby. It was frozen over. Crowds of people were round the pool, boys skimming stones to make a long twanging noise, and far out near the island big men on proper ice skates whizzed round bending forward with hands clasped behind their backs. Ducks came waddling and skidding over the ice before splashing into the water for thrown bread.

Something was happening among the black frozen reeds. People were all looking.

Really loud I shouted out, 'Help, there's a man in the water, help, he's drowning.'

An American soldier flung off his jerkin, kicked his shoes away and passed me his army cap.

'Here, take care of this for me,' and near the wall he lowered himself into the water and waded towards the man, pushing aside sheets of ice. The drowning man bent his head under the water; he didn't seem to want to come out. With help from other men he was pulled onto the bank wrestling with the soldier and swearing.

'Come on, we're going home,' said Dad, all cross.

'But we've only just come.'

'Do as I say come on.'

'But I'm looking after his cap.'

'Never mind the damn cap,' and he threw it down near the struggling soldier.

Why didn't the man want to be rescued and why was Dad so cross, not speaking as he dragged us back over the fields. What had I done wrong? I was the one who told everybody about it and I wanted to give the soldier his cap back. I hated grown ups. All of them.

In the art class we made a poster with CS in capital letters. CS was short for Children's Shelter. If a child was out playing when the siren went off they could look for a window with CS, knock on the door and go in till the All Clear came. I decorated my poster with ivy winding round the letters, stuck gold stars on, put it in our front window and waited. Nobody came to the door. We never used the gas masks, Dad didn't need the bayonet in the top cupboard from the First World War where grandpa was killed, and no German spies came. War was going to be no fun at all.

Across the road was the Progress shoe factory. Every day at half past twelve the factory hooter sounded, the whirr of machinery stopped, and workers hurried home for dinner. Some on bikes, others forming a two by two procession, half running, half quick walking to various houses where meals were waiting. Later they all rushed back to reach the factory before the hooter for half past one. That hooter was also our signal to return to school.

One hot Friday afternoon I set off to school early with Eileen to give us time to play in the field in the sun. Mam gave instructions. 'Now listen for the Progress hooter and as soon as you hear it go back to school.'

Bent's field, shaped with folds and hollows, just off the main street was white with daises and Eileen showed me how to make a daisy chain. First you pick a bunch of flowers with the thickest stalks and put them in a heap before settling onto a grassy bank. With a finger nail you split the stalk half way along to make a gap; then through this gap you pushed another stalk as far as the head of the daisy. You made a gap in that stalk, then another, then another till you had a chain.

'The hooter's a long time going,' said Eileen, busy with her chains. 'Let's listen.'

There was no sound of walkers in the street, no bicycle bells, just the whirr of the factory. 'I think we've missed it,' I said, 'they've gone in, we'll be late.'

But neither of us moved and I said we'd never get there in time and don't let's go to school at all. It was Friday anyway.

'How will we know when to go home?'

'We'll listen for the others and then pretend we went to school.'

'What about the daisy chains?'

'We'll have to leave them here,' I said.

And so we did, sitting all afternoon on that green bank with the white daisies.

When we heard children in the street we went home leaving all our beautiful daisy chains in the field.

Something was wrong. Mother had a strange look about her.

'Where've you been?'

'To school of course.'

'Oh, no, you haven't, young lady. Sit in this chair, put this nightie on and go straight to bed. I've had the school boardman here. I've never been so ashamed, never thought that man would come to our house.'

The school boardman! 'That's the boardman,' children would whisper as he rode by on his bike in his official cap. His job was to check that all children went to school and he'd called at the juniors on the one and only day that I had ever played truant. Mother knelt in front of me pulling off my shoes.

'You young madam, making me feel a fool, bringing disgrace on this house. I don't know what your dad will say, off to bed this minute, go on, out of my sight, you wicked, wicked girl.'

And off to bed I went, in broad daylight with nothing to do for hours except to think about the dreadful thing I had done, the shame I'd brought to my mother and the daisy chains.

IV
GRAMMAR SCHOOL 1943 - 1946

'My name is Sylvia and my Dad's a doctor,' announced the girl in front, turning round; dark hair, blue eyes, rosy cheeks, lovely face.

It was my first day at grammar school.

That was a strange boastful thing Sylvia said but everything was strange anyway.

Boys at the school were not called Peter, Timothy or Clive but Williams, Robinson or Mason. Older pupils looked like grown-up men and women to me. Classes were called forms. Girls wore green tunics and everybody carried leather satchels full of exciting school equipment like protractors and set squares.

'Copy down this timetable, homework in the last column.' Hist, Geog, Fr, Biol, Chem, Phys, Eng lit, Eng Lang and PE.

Coalville Grammar School, the official grammar school for the county area, was twelve miles away from the village. Grammar schools in Leicester were only four miles away but you had to pay fees to go there even if you had passed the scholarship exam. Margaret Brent, a friend who lived near the blacksmiths, was at Newark Girls Grammar school in Leicester and learned Latin. She taught me some.

'Caesar had some jam for tea
Give us some said Anthony.'
If you say it loud that's Latin.
Mus erat sub mensa
Murem capio volo
Igitur ego sub mensa.

This is Latin for:
'The mouse is under the table
I want to capture the mouse
Therefore I am under the table.'

The school bus for Coalville, a place I had never visited before, rarely arrived at school in time for morning assembly and it left at four o'clock. Because we lived in a village quite far away, we could not stay behind for after-school activities such as tennis. At the end of the first day at school I got off two stops early so all the village would see me in my tunic and green blazer with a gold badge saying 'Virtu et Vide' That was Latin.

As a present for passing the scholarship, Mam and Dad gave David and me fountain pen sets. Mine was green and his was blue. Conway Stuart was the name on the box and under the lid was a pen and propelling pencil each in separate velvet compartments. The pen and pencil were mottled green with shiny bands of gold round the cap and edge of the pen, and the top and tip of the pencil. Inside the pen was a rubber tube which you squeezed to suck up the ink. It was a beautiful present, much nicer than any birthday or Christmas present I'd ever had.

Lots of newcomers arrived in the village.

'There's an evacuee at church and her name's Patalegs,' I said.

'It's not Patalegs,' David said. 'Her name's Pat Alexander.'

A German spy moved into a wooden bungalow down West Street. We knew he was a spy because he didn't speak to anybody that proved he couldn't speak English.

David said we were stupid because German spies don't keep greyhounds and David had heard him in the co-op speaking with a cockney accent. Dad said any man who talked with a cockney accent and kept greyhounds was a crook and we children were to keep out of his way. Through the front window we watched the man strolling arm in arm with his wife to the paper shop. He was short with black hair and side burns and she wore a flowered dress that swung from side to side as she walked. Her hair was auburn in floppy curls and she laughed and smiled all the time. She was lovely, like Rita Hayworth.

'Come away from the window,' Mam said, 'have nothing to do with them. She looks like a showgirl to me. White high heels in the morning. Listen, all of you, if they speak to you don't answer.'

Learning French was a worry. How could anybody learn every word of another language; it would be impossible. Perhaps the letters were different, perhaps A was C in French like a code.

Dad said, 'When you start learning French can you teach it to me each night when you come home?'

Hockey was frightening, standing in a muddy field in the cold waiting to be killed by a hard red ball. When you hit it with a hockey stick it sent a jarring shock right up to your shoulders. You could get your legs banged even with shin pads on. I had to write my own sick notes. The teacher said, 'Mary what is a mulcifrated back?' 'I don't know Miss.'

Girls who'd been excused games had to stay in the cloakroom and one morning the headmaster announced, 'A purse was stolen from the cloakroom yesterday. In my office I wish to see Mary Rogers and Sheila Baines.'

We both waited outside his door, Sheila went in first. I knew I hadn't taken it and I'd be late for my lesson. After a long while Mr Glister, the headmaster, came out said, 'I don't need to see you Mary.' Sheila must have owned up. The theft was not mentioned again by the headmaster. Sheila was a goody goody, I was not. The whole school must have thought I was the thief. I felt terrible.

Another worry was school dinners. I had free dinners and every Monday when the money was collected I had to go up to the desk with my brother and say so.

After school one day I wandered down West Street in our village. I could tell which was their bungalow because there were big wire netting cages behind the hedge. The wooden bungalows were raised on stilts and the woman was perched on the top step smoking and swaying to dance music. Then she saw me, gave a wide smile and called, 'Hello love, come here and keep me company.'

Standing at the gate I called back, 'Please can I take a dog for walk.'

'Oh, darling,' she said, 'you don't take greys for walks they have exercise every day on the track.'

'Well, can I feed one then?'

'Oh, no dearie, they have special feed. Everything has to be weighed.'

'Well can I see them then?'

Blowing smoke through orange lips she paused and then said, 'Come next Monday same time. My husband will be here then. I'll ask him to let you see them.'

I waited, if I looked sad she might change her mind. 'What's your name darling?'

'Mary and I'm nearly eleven and I go to grammar school.'

In the upper hall we learned to dance The Lancers in a class called Social Graces. Dinners were also in the upstairs dining hall; each form at their own tables. After lots of noisy chatter and rattle of cutlery came silence for grace.

'For what we are about to receive may the Lord make us truly thankful. Amen.'

I was truly thankful; it tasted nicer than dinner at home. One boy sat alone at a small table with a special knife and fork.

He was Jewish and the boys laughed at him not because he was Jewish but because he wrote stories for children. He didn't seem to mind; he laughed with them. On the long bus journey he told me he prayed every day with something with a funny name strapped to his head. He showed me a new invention from Switzerland; a heavy black pen that did not need ink and had no nib. It wrote fast and could even write upside down. He said it cost over five pounds; the name on it was Biro.

Teachers wore black gowns that slipped off their shoulders when they lifted an arm to write on the board and had to keep hitching them up. The lessons were good, Physics with the jumping iron filings and the balance scales with a funny German name. These scales were kept in a glass case away from dust. The weights looked like bits of bent tin. We played with an amazing substance called mercury, which rolled round on the table in small silver balls and you could press it into lots of smaller balls and it could never be destroyed. I took some home to play with once, wrapped in brown paper and tried to melt it in a dish on the fire. I wrote down what happened but the teacher didn't seem interested when I showed her the notes.

In Geometry we learned about Isosceles and his triangle but Archimedes principle was nothing special. It stands to reason if you drop a big stone in a jar of water, the water level will rise. When the stone's taken out, the water falls to fill the same space as the big stone.

At the end of an Algebra class Miss Hoyle asked if anybody had any questions.

I put my hand up and said, 'Miss what is the purpose of Algebra?'

She told me off in front of the class for being impudent – I really wanted to know, she didn't answer the question. I felt silly.

The boys never got told off. 'Don't you have doors in your house Jones?'

'Yes Miss but we have butlers to shut 'em.'

The man wasn't there when I arrived on Monday and she took me into the sitting room to wait for him on a frilly chair and drink lemonade while we listened to Frank Sinatra on the wireless. All along the fireplace shelf were lipsticks and powder puffs and ashtrays and curlers. There was a fancy box with a funny word on it.

'What's in that box?' She said it was greasepaint, stage make-up and, standing in front of a mirror, she took out two sticks and showed me how she put it on.

'Number 9 to catch the lights and then number 7 to mask the yellow. Blend them together, see.' Spreading the greasepaint on her cheeks she said, 'You just use your finger tips and try not to make a line.'

She looked lovely, all bright and colourful with red cheeks like a doll, none of the other women in the village looked like her. While I stretched my mouth wide and tilted my head back she drew round my lips with the carmine greasepaint that smelt like candle wax. Afterwards she lit a Craven A cigarette with a proper lighter and showed me how to hold it. 'Keep the arm raised up and wide so the smoke doesn't go in your hair, you don't want your hair to smell of tobacco. Go on, you try, hold it. Oh, listen, pass it back, this is Victor Sylvester, come on, let's quick step.'

Then a man's voice shouted above the music, 'Are you there, Velia?'

'He's here. He's back,' she whispered, turning the music off, 'wait outside till he's ready.'

Her name was Velia.

He hardly spoke when he showed me round. Each of the five dogs had its own long roofed in cage. There were two wire doors at each entrance and we had to walk in the first one and shut it behind us before opening the second; that was in case they ran out. On the ground were piles of brown dog dirt; first he collected it on a pan then he swilled the ground with something in a bucket that smelt worse than the dog dirt, it was called Jeyes Fluid.

One dog came up to me straight away, and pushed its nose under my chin. It was light brown mottled with paler brown underneath. The eyes were like two dark marbles and when I stroked the long head I could feel the bone underneath. Its legs were like sticks of iron.

'What's its name?' I asked.

'This bitch is Lady of Westminster and she's werf a bandle.'

I practised saying it to myself while we went to the other cages, 'She's werf a bandle.'

I followed him to the other cages but every time I turned round Lady of Westminster was watching me.

When I went home Mam said, 'What's that on your lips?'

Just in time I remembered the carmine stuff and said, 'I've been practising for the school play.'

Early in the first term at Grammar School all the new girls were directed to the gymnasium for a special lecture called Hygiene. Wearing our white blouses under green box-pleated tunics we waited in subdued rows between the high walls of the gym with its woody smells.

A nice lady doctor, with grey hair and wearing a brown check suit, hung up some charts with picture of female insides and pointed out such things as ovaries and fallopian tubes. We didn't have to write anything down. She talked about something called menstruation and how to deal with it. It wasn't very interesting. Then she told us about eggs and sperm and showed us a picture of a baby inside a lady. Using words like testicles and penis she explained what married people did together in bed and finished by announcing, 'And that is the true meaning of the word love. Are there any questions?'

Questions! I looked round. Surely nobody would ask a question about such personal and embarrassing things.

Nobody spoke at first and then a girl stood up and asked, 'Does every girl have periods?'

'Every normal girl does,' replied the doctor.

What? What? Every girl? Oh my goodness, that could mean me. I gestured to the girl next to me, 'Us?' She nodded. How horrible. 'Boys as well?' 'No' and she shook her head. What a worry, and I hadn't been listening properly.

At home, desperately trying to sound casual, I waited till Dad went into the kitchen and said to Mam, 'We had a lesson about monthly periods today.'

'Oh, I could have told you about that,' she replied.

A long time later when I started she said, 'Never talk about this sort of thing, especially to men, they don't like it.'

In Year One I won the French prize and on Speech Day morning we all went to the local cinema for a rehearsal. When I walked across the stage some girls laughed. My friend said there was a hole in my black stocking. Mam came in the afternoon; that was the only time she came to Coalville because it was such a long way away. She wore a cream coat and a cream beret and looked smart. The prize was a grey book called *A Girl's Duty* by Ursula Vivian with the school badge stamped on the front.

'That's a nice-looking girl,' Mam commented about a new pupil from Ceylon. She didn't seem anything special to me but her younger sister was really lovely with long black hair in ringlets, big dark eyes, rosebud shaped red lips and a brown complexion. When she first appeared in the assembly hall, wearing a flowered dress because her uniform was on order, everybody stared at her. She stood looking down at the floor and did not seem to know she was beautiful. In the whole school she was the only girl with a brown skin.

I went to see the dogs nearly every day after changing out of my school uniform. Of course I had to make up things to tell Mam so she didn't know where I'd been. I said I'd been doing homework with friends or collecting wild flowers for the nature class.

After a few visits the man let me count the dog biscuits into a tin dish and give them out, they gobbled them up. He still didn't talk much.

'I wish I had a pet dog,' I said one day,' then I could take it for a walk.'

'Pets? They ain't pets,' he said, 'them dogs is ranners.' That was another word to practise saying.

What I wanted most was for my friends to see me with a greyhound but he told me somebody collected them every day for exercise.

'Perhaps they'd like a walk as well,' I said, but he wasn't listening as usual.

One afternoon while she was showing me how she painted her toe nails by first pushing bits of cotton wool between each toe Velia said, 'We came away from the bombs in London because I lost the baby.' She stopped doing her nails and looked sad when she said it but she soon smiled again.

That same afternoon I must have worn him down with talk of taking a dog out because he said,

'You could take her up the lane,' and he lifted a leather strap from its hook, fastened it onto her collar and guided her through the double mesh doors. I daren't speak in case he changed his mind. He wrapped the lead round my wrist twice then put the loop in my hand.

'Keep the lead like this all the time, never, never let go. She's werf a bandle.'

I wanted people to think it was my dog but there was no one about so I took her into a field. I had to take my cardigan off to sit on the grass. I pulled one arm out of the sleeve but while I was changing the lead to my other hand she tugged at it and before I could do anything she was loose.

Up the field she ran; I didn't know anything could run so fast. With the lead flying behind she was soon a black streak in the distance. I chased after her screaming, 'Come back Lady, come back. Please, please come back.'

She raced through the hedge and uphill into the barley field and out of sight. 'Come back,' I yelled, so out of breath the words wouldn't come. I had the stitch and dropped to the ground crying in pain and very frightened. I'd lost his best greyhound. I daren't go home. He'd find me. What would a London crook do to a child who'd let go of the lead? I prayed. 'Please Jesus, make her come back.'

It was beginning to get dark as I sat gulping sobs and wondering what to do, when something pushed me from behind. She was back - Lady of Westminster was back. Hardly daring to move a muscle I slid my hand slowly along the grass till it touched the lead then grabbed it, first with one hand, then the other.

'Oh, you bad, bad dog,' but she just lay there panting with her long tongue flopping out sideways. I wiped the slobber from her mouth with my cardigan, picked the barley seeds from her coat and hurried back.

They were both waiting at the gate. He was cross. 'Where the 'ell have you been?'

'I lost my way, I didn't know the time, I'm very sorry.'

Bending forward he ran his hand over her coat and underneath.

'This bitch is 'ot. She's been ranning,' but I had my story ready.

'She ran round me in a circle on the lead in the field, she ran a lot of times.'

He believed me and said, 'Oh, she'd like that - you can take her out again tomorrow.'

I didn't know what to say because I dare not take her again.

At home Mam was listening to the wireless and knitting.

'Where d'you think you've been young lady, till this time?'

'Just with my friends.'

'Well get upstairs this minute. It's past your bedtime and we want a bit of peace.'

Changing the subject I said, 'How can you lose a baby? A baby's not that small.'

She stopped knitting, switched the wireless off and said, 'What do you mean?'

'I heard a woman say she'd lost a baby.'

'That's grown up talk young lady, and not for your ears. Who was it?'

'Oh, just somebody.'

'It's not that woman down the back lane is it?'

And, before I could answer she said, 'I wasn't born yesterday. I'm not daft. We know where you go every night. And you're not going again.'

David was not on the school bus coming home and he was still not home when Dad came from work and getting dark so Dad went to the phone box to ring the police.

It turned out my brother David had been kept in for detention and had walked twelve miles home because he had no money. Dad wrote to the headmaster in his nice handwriting, first dipping the pen in the ink then waving his arm at the beginning of each word. At the end of the letter he put, 'I beg to remain Sir, your obedient servant W Rogers.'

Mr Glister replied that in future bus pupils would serve their detentions at dinner times but in any case David should have asked the office for money to get home. We knew that even if he'd thought about it he was too shy to ask for money.

My school tunic was not the same as other girls. Theirs was made of heavy material, dark green and shiny, mine was a thinner cloth, Mam had made it. She had also dyed some white shoes to make them black, but the white showed through. We did get a clothing allowance for uniform from the Education department but some of it was used for clothes for the rest of the family.

For summer the uniform was a green dress in check gingham. One hot summer afternoon wearing our check dresses the whole school had to sit round in the playing field watching the boys in a cricket match. It was a long afternoon to watch a dull cricket match and a friend who lived in Coalville said she knew the way to creep out through some allotments and into town then we could come back before home time.

Next morning Mr Glister announced, 'Two girls from this school were seen hurrying through some allotments yesterday. Will Mary Rogers and Betty Whatnall see me afterwards.'

In trouble again.

Meadow Sweet with its flowers like frothy clouds and smell of summer bordered the Anstey brook where I learned to swim. 'Just lie on your back and float on the water.' How could anything as heavy as a person float on water, you'd just sink and drown. Paddling felt nice at first, wading through darting tiddlers and bursts of mud, but in the deep I didn't like the feel of stones and funny things swirling round my feet.

The deepest part of all was called the Pole because a tree trunk stretched from one side to the other; big boys sat on it and pushed each other in.

Mam came with us once carrying sandwiches and towels but we had to move when the cows came because Mam was frightened of them. She was frightened of lots of things especially thunder storms, she was always worried when the sky went dark. 'Listen, can you hear thunder?' She used to make us sit watching the lightning through the window, 'Look at the pretty sky,' then she'd go and hide under the stairs with ear plugs in and a tin washing up bowl on her head. We knew where she was. She was frightened of air raid sirens and afraid of water. She could not swim.

One Saturday morning I went on the bus with Eileen to Vestry Street baths in Leicester for the first time. We changed in a proper changing room called a cubicle and then put our clothes in a basket and took it to a lady. The water was bright green with a fresh clean, chemical smell.

An old woman with a humped back was teaching a boy to swim. He was in the water with a rope tied round his waist and she walked along the side pulling the rope. If somebody held a rope I think I could learn to swim. While I stood at the side Eileen, who was tough and not frightened of anything, jumped in, swam to the other end, then turned and came back, wiping her eyes with a wet hand and so out of breath she could hardly speak.

'Oh Mary,' she stammered looking up at me, 'ain't it lovely. I ain't never going in the brook again.'

My birthdays were not special days because I was born on December the twenty-seventh and it was too close to Christmas. Presents were usually labelled 'For Christmas and your birthday.'

In the first term at grammar school I'd invited three friends, Audrey, Norma and Sheila to my party. There had been arguments with Mam who said they would not come all the way from Coalville on a Sunday afternoon in winter. I really looked forward to them coming to my house. I wanted Mam and Dad to see them and I wanted to show them my bedroom. I waited and waited at the Glenfield Turn till it was getting late and I was cold but they didn't come so I walked home in tears. We were going to have tea in the front room with tinned peaches and pink blancmange.

All the family was disappointed but Mam opened the front window and called to two girls who were walking by, 'Ask your mother if you can come to a birthday party.' They came.

When school started after the holidays I asked Norma why she didn't come and she said she forgot. I didn't ask the other two.

Saturday mornings were an adventure, going alone to Leicester on Hilton and Dawsons bus. At the hospital on Groby Road men got on wearing pale blue berets and blue uniforms that looked like pyjamas. They were wounded soldiers and when they offered their fare to the conductor he waved it away; that was because they had fought for us in the war.

There were lots of uniformed men in Leicester. Ordinary soldiers in khaki jerkins, side caps and trousers made of rough material and airmen in Airforce blue. I felt sorry for the sailors; they had to run through the town dodging women who were chasing them to touch their collars for luck. American servicemen wore tailored beige uniforms and looked very smart. People walked close behind to hear them talking just like in the films.

First treat was the hot peas man and I waited while he set up his stall in the market place on a bare wooden table. Onto a gas ring he lifted a white enamel bucket full of soaked peas, lit the flame with a match and heated them up while I stood close to warm my hands. A pile of saucers, all different colours were laid out and two or three spoons tied with chains to the counter. I handed over the sixpence, he filled a saucer, I shook a few drops of vinegar on them and set to. They tasted wonderful, especially on cold mornings.

The market-place smelt lovely with pyramids of apples and vegetables. Peaches were on sale in the market, each one separately nestled in blue tissue, I had only ever seen them before in tins. They were the size of apples but with a yellowy skin like suede with a blush of rouge. An American soldier asked the price and it was two shillings. Two shillings for one peach. The American asked for five. I watched the trader's face, he didn't look surprised at all but when he turned away to get some brown paper bags I saw him smile to himself. A crowd had gathered to stare as the soldier opened his wallet and handed over a ten shilling note. Ten shillings just for peaches.

In the fish market you could buy kittens, puppies, baby rabbits, kid goats, hens and day old chicks, bright yellow and fluffy. The chicks were squashed together in a flat cardboard box cheeping and climbing over each other. Dangling closely overhead were electric light bulbs to keep them warm. Everybody crowded round and children pushed to the front pointing out any dead ones for the man to throw in the bucket. I wished I could have taken a chicken home to look after but Dad said it would die.

The lift at the department store, Lewis's, was full and the uniformed attendant announced, 'Are there any children without their parents in this lift?' 'Yes, I am.' She laughed, 'You're not a child,' and pressed the button. I was twelve and suddenly felt grown up.

We were standing in a line at school wearing our gym kit when Miss Smith, the short, strict teacher, who walked on the back of her heels, called my friend Hazel to the front where everybody could see her. I thought she'd done something wrong as usual.

'Now, look carefully at the way Hazel stands with her head up, shoulders back, tummy in, bottom tucked in and balancing slightly forward. Now, all of you stand like Hazel and I'm coming round to inspect each one. I tried standing straight, tummy in but it was hard to do for long and I soon flopped down again.

Hazel was tall and thin with long legs, sparkly eyes and short untidy dark hair. Teachers did not like her. In the music lesson she was told off for singing words to an exercise instead of la la. *Every minute he gets bolder, now he's leaning on my shoulder, Ma, he's kissing me.*

And it was Hazel who asked if we could quickstep at the lunch time dances instead of the Veleta. 'Certainly not,' was the answer. In class she flirted with the boys turning round to laugh with them; she didn't sit still like other girls and always seemed to be shuffling about.

One Friday instead of going back to Ellistown, Hazel came home with me on the school bus to stay for the weekend. The young conservatives were holding a dance in the school hall on Saturday night; we were going together and Dad would meet us afterwards to walk us home. In the afternoon Hazel tried to teach me the quickstep but my feet wouldn't move properly.

It didn't seem a bit like the hall of my infants' school; everything looked different as we sat listening to the band and watching couples dancing. Places change according to the people in them. Then the floor cleared and everybody stood at the side to watch Little Billy, a midget, dancing with petite Dot Smart, a lovely lady from the village. Billy in a navy pin striped suit with his hair plastered down smiled up at Mrs Smart in her green crepe dress that wafted out as he steered her round in a

waltz. People clapped when they'd finished and Billy, looking so proud, bowed to everybody before leading Mrs Smart by the hand back to her husband's table.

The next dance was a quickstep and Hazel soon had a partner. While I stood at the side I watched her dance quicksteps, waltzes and fox trots one after another, a different boy each time.

It was a special evening. One by one girls were picked out from the dance floor to stand at the front and finally one was chosen as Young Conservatives Princess. Photographers from a magazine called *Picture Post* were taking pictures as she was being crowned.

At home that night we lay awake talking over the exciting events of the evening when Hazel asked if I'd ever kissed a boy.

'Lots of times,' I said.

'Come into my bed and I'll show you how to kiss properly.'

She kissed me on the lips under the covers and then pushed me away. 'You've given yourself away. I can tell you've never done any kissing have you?'

I wondered how she knew.

Next morning when Mam found us in the same bed she was really angry. Later in the kitchen she whispered, 'You must not sleep with her, there is TB in her family. Why do you think I made up two beds? TB is catching.'

What excitement when *Picture Post* came out! Page after page of people at the dance in our village. The crowned princess, men in the band and, on one whole page, a head and shoulder photo of Hazel laughing while she danced. Underneath it said, 'The girl the Tories overlooked.' Two years later she died.

The next time there was a dance in the village school it was interrupted by an announcement. 'Ladies and Gentlemen. Good news. The war is over.'

Everyone shouted 'Hurray' at the top of their voices, the band played the National Anthem and we all sang. Then we danced the Conga, in a long line through the hall down the corridor and back again. One girl stood alone by a wall. 'Why is Lavinia crying?

'Because the Americans will go back.'

When Uncle Ron came home from Borneo or wherever he was, Mam tied balloons on the front door and a notice saying,

'Welcome Home, Ron.'

Jack Cutter was a handsome man with a thin moustache and when he came back he told his wife she was too old and ugly for him.

There she sat in the middle of the second row, waiting for the concert to begin, the most astounding girl I'd ever seen. About my age with dark loosely curled hair gently falling to her shoulders, dark eyes, clear complexion and a beautiful profile.

And here she was, in our village at a Young Conservatives concert in the church hall, sitting so calmly, hands in her lap almost hidden by the embroidered cuffs of her soft cream suit. At first, chatting with friends I had not noticed her until I looked round.

Her stillness and serenity was amazing. She sat upright, half smiling, in her chair, never turning her head one way or the other as the concert proceeded. A soprano was singing, 'Little Polly Perkins' but I could not take my eyes from the girl. I was enthralled and wished she would turn round and look at me.

I nudged my friend who whispered, 'French, staying with the Lacey family, penfriend,' I'd never seen a foreign person before and asked what her name was. 'Gabriella.' Gabriella, what a beautiful name.

I wanted a pen-friend but did not know how to find one. Studying the map of France in my school album I chose a place

called Abbeville that was not too far away from England. I wrote a letter in French. 'To the proprietor of any newspaper in Abbeville,' asking if they could find me a pen-friend. About a week later came a reply in a blue crinkly envelope lined with fine paper.

'I am the daughter of the newspaper who your (sic) write and wish to become a pen-friend.' Her name was Genevieve and she sent a photograph of herself, dark curly hair and a nice face, tilted on one side. She didn't look like Gabriella.

One evening at home Mam said, 'What would you think if I was having another baby?'

I said 'OK, if it's a girl,' and carried on with my homework pretending I was thinking no more about it.

Night after night Mam was sewing baby clothes on the treadle machine and we talked about names for girls. Sometimes she kept me at home from school for company. Then I had to stay away for a few weeks.

On the day the baby was due, Dad was at home and when a nurse came, Mam told me to go round to Dot Smart's house up the road. I sat in the chair watching her combing her dark curly hair in the mirror over the fireplace. We talked about a lot of things but not about the baby and what was happening at home. I wanted her to tell me about that. Later on Dad came for me and said, 'You can come home now, Mam's had the baby.'

'What is it?'

'A little boy.'

My heart sank. Mam was sitting up in bed. On two chairs was a drawer and the nurse was tucking the baby in. Such a tiny child with a squashy red face and dainty dark eyebrows.

'Don't be too disappointed,' she said, 'he's a lovely little brother and his name is Guy Stuart.'

'Can I go back to school now and see my friends?'

It was another three weeks before I went back to school. That night my green tunic and clean white blouse were laid out on the bed and I could hardly sleep for excitement at going back to school.

When teachers asked me why I'd been away I told them Mam needed help with a new baby. Somebody was sitting in my place in class and I had to sit at the back, away from my friends and next to girls who always got low marks. What a worry. One of them was a girl named Marjorie Rodgers and when the next list for English went up on the board I had two out of ten and Marjorie had nine out of ten. Marjorie said:

'My gran will be pleased with that mark.' Marjorie was on report and needed to improve.

Next day when our papers were returned I had nine marks and Marjorie had two. The teacher had mixed us up. Marjorie wouldn't say anything because it would upset her grandma and I daren't tell the teacher she'd made a mistake.

English lessons were easy to catch up with but I soon learnt it was impossible to catch up with science and French. I hated being at the bottom and began to lose interest in schoolwork.

On a summer evening about that time there was the excitement of a fairground in a field at Anstey opposite the pack horse bridge. There was loud waltzing organ music, swing boats higher and higher, prancing, colourful horses and the nasty smell of burning oil from the engine. A young man with a scowl and dirty clothes jumped from dodgem to dodgem collecting fares. Me, in my new brown blouse and matching skirt, and my friend Sheila, were posing at the side trying to be noticed.

After a while, over on the other side of the dodgems a man stood leaning against his bike looking my way. I moved away and still he was there staring. Oh, a man taking notice. I surely must look nice.

Already separated from Sheila I pushed through the crowds but he was following me. He likes me. He looked about twenty one with a serious expression and staring blue eyes. I watched people trying to hook rubber rings over jars of goldfish, conscious that he was watching me.

The man came closer and asked, 'Can you tell me the way to Leicester?' I began to explain but he interrupted, 'Show me.'

We left the fairground together; I walked alongside as he pushed his bike by the wide grass verge. The fairground organ music sounded even nicer outside the ground. Lights flashed in the darkness and there were lots of people about. He stopped, laid his bike down on the grass, gently laid me on the ground and then he was lying on top of me.

I wasn't sure if it was right but I didn't want him to think I was silly. He kissed me. Oh, this is what happens, I thought it was nice. Then his hands were all over my new blouse and I was angry. How dare he touch my new blouse. Then he was undoing my buttons. Somewhere somebody screamed and screamed. It was me. Looking up a gang of local boys surrounded us, 'What's going off?' one of them said. I knew the leader, tall with tight curly hair. The man jumped up to get to his bike. The boys surrounded him. I stood up, trembling and turning to fasten my blouse.

The leader grabbed the bike while two boys gripped the man's arms; one each side. He looked scared.

'Clear off,' the leader yelled, throwing the bike at him, 'Clear off and don't ever come back.'

Afterwards I walked home with Sheila and told her about it. Of course I didn't tell Mam, I never told Mam anything.

When I got home from school one day Mam was crying. A few months earlier a gypsy woman had come to the door and when Mam would not buy anything the gypsy said, 'That's because you're mean. If you weren't mean you'd buy yourself some new teeth.'

After that Mam had all her teeth taken out and she'd had to wait a few weeks for the gums to settle. Now the new ones had come and she hated them. 'I'll never look nice again,' she said and started crying again.

Mam and Dad were planning to exchange our rented house in the village for a six-bedroom house in Leicester, where they could take in lodgers. I was unhappy at school and liked the idea of helping Mam run the boarding-house. My job would be to look after my baby brother and help Mam while Dad carried on with his own job as a wages clerk.

When we began to live in Leicester I missed my friends from the village. The house, on Uppingham Road, had no garden and I spent afternoons taking Guy to the park.

One day a man with curly grey hair came up to me and said politely, 'Is that your child?' When I said he was my brother he asked if I would like to go to Brighton with him for the weekend. I was so frightened and, not knowing what to say, I just said, 'Yes.' He said to meet him on Saturday morning at eleven outside the Post Office.

All that day I stayed in worrying about it. A few days later I was horrified to see him sitting upstairs on my bus reading a paper. He turned round and asked why I hadn't turned up. When I told him I had not felt well he didn't seem to mind and carried on reading.

I was still writing to Genevieve and she was always asking me to visit her in France. When Mam and Dad finally said I could go I started a Saturday job at Lewis's, a big department store in Leicester, to save up enough money for the journey.

Dad gave my brother a ten-shilling note to see me safely onto the boat train at Victoria station in London. To make conversation with the couple in the small compartment I asked what time we would be at Boulogne. After telling me they looked at each other and giggled. I must have said it wrong. I felt silly.

I knew French people kissed each other when they met but it was embarrassing when Genevieve kissed me on both sides of my face. Genevieve wore a summer dress that was too tight across the bust. Madame Lafosse, a lady who spoke English, was waiting with her and travelled with us back to Abbeville. On the train Madame Lafosse gave me a bottle of perfume called Je Reviens by Worth. I knew it meant 'I shall return.' After opening the beautiful blue packet I drew out the frosted glass bottle and eased off the glass stopper. The lovely smooth, flowery smell filled the carriage.

Madame explained that Genevieve's father had given his bicycle to Monsieur Lafosse to escape from the Germans and she would do anything for Genevieve's family. I was surprised when she asked me if I was Catholic, the first time anyone had ever spoken about religion to me. When I said no she told me not to mention it to anybody. 'When Genevieve goes to mass just stand at the side.'

From the station to Genevieve's house, we picked our way through rubble, stepping over blocks of stone from the bombed church. The house had a printing works in the back yard. Genevieve's parents were old and every night after dinner her fat father, with his white wispy hair said, *'Bonne nuit'* and disappeared upstairs.

Genevieve's mother, a big lady with dark hair tied back, wore an apron all the time. French food was very strange, the mother had no idea how to fry eggs on the huge black cooking range. She stirred them up into basin with a fork and I wanted a proper fried egg. One morning I waited till she'd cracked an egg in the basin and then I was going to say, *'Pardonez moi, madame,'* before showing her how to fry my egg. That was the plan but in jumping up I knocked over cups of tea and spilt them. I felt awful.

Every morning after breakfast I taught Genevieve how to smoke. She wasn't much good at it.

Our bedroom was massive with flimsy curtains hanging everywhere inside the room. From our beds we called across to each other trying to think of boys' names that were laughable in French and in English. I suggested Marmaduke and Archibald but they were not funny in French. She said some names that I didn't think were amusing then we discovered the name Claude which was pronounced *Clod* in French. At last we had found a name that was funny in both languages and could not sleep for giggling. *'Bonne nuit, Clod'*, 'Good Night, Claude.'

Shops in France were amazing. Row upon row of sweets arranged in windows like works of art. At first it looked like fruit but the blackberries and raspberries were boiled sweets and the miniature peaches, grapes and bananas arranged in paper frills that looked like lace were made of marzipan. I had left a country of shortages and rationing and here I was with all this. And we had won the war.

When you went into a shop you had to say, *'Bonjour Madame.'*

I bought sweets in francs and nobody looked surprised when I spoke in French. I soon got into the sing-song of the words, *'bonjour madame,' 'au revoir madame.'*

An emerald green cotton scarf printed all over with bands of tiny flower petals cost a lot of francs but it was so beautiful I had to buy it.

My grandfather was killed in France at the battle of the Somme. Dad was eight years old at the time and he was keen, while I was in France, for me to visit the grave he had never seen.

After three changes at dreary stations we arrived at a village called Bethune. The cemetery was lovely, acres of green with white neat headstones all in straight lines. Row on row. The rows kept changing as we walked past and saw them from different angles.

'Look for Lieutenant W. Rogers,' Dad had said. 'Your grandpa was promoted from sergeant on the battlefield when other officers were killed.'

I stood at the grave looking down.

Presently I whispered, 'I am your grand-daughter, you are my grandfather.'

But I felt nothing.

Spreading my beautiful scarf over a corner of the headstone I photographed the grave. *Lt W S Rogers. Notts and Derby Regiment, killed August 1916.*

In a café afterwards Genevieve ordered a piece of cheese and as soon as it was placed on the table half a dozen flies landed on it. It was disgusting. Genevieve cut a piece and ate it. Remembering mother's words, 'It will be strange, just do what they do,' I did the same.

On the rattly train going back something felt sticky, I was bleeding, had nothing with me and didn't know the French words to tell my friend. All I could say was stomach ache; she didn't understand. I felt terrible. I went to the smelly toilet on the train, where there was no seat, just two places to put your feet. Folding my lovely scarf into a square I put it in my knickers. Later, in Genevieve's kitchen I threw it on the fire. At least I had a photograph of it.

It seemed a very long time to be away from home for two whole weeks even though I had managed to cut the holiday short by two days. People were always asking if I had 'ennui' meaning homesickness. I was really miserable. When at last the day came to return Madame Lafosse again came with us to Boulogne and waited at the quayside.

'Madame, why is Genevieve crying?'

'Because she doesn't want you to go.'

'Why?'

Putting her face close to mine she said, very deliberately, 'She likes you.'

It felt strange that somebody would cry because I was going away.

Sometimes a school friend would come to Leicester all the way from Coalville to stay overnight but I had no friends nearby until I joined a youth club and met June who was tall, fair and never hurried anywhere. June's mother wiped her hand on her apron before shaking hands with me but there was still cold dust on it.

June worked in a factory and on Saturday nights we went to dances at Cossington Street baths except when I had to stay in and babysit while Mam and Dad went out.

'It's our turn to go out this Saturday,' Mam would say.

June's mother told her I should not be staying in babysitting because I was only young once and it was not my baby. I thought about that and wished I could have a job and earn money but mostly I didn't want to be at home all day.

Worrying in case Mam would be cross I practised what I would say and how I would say it. While she was peeling potatoes one morning and I was polishing silver I said quietly, 'I wish I could go to work like other girls.'

Expecting an argument I waited for the answer.

'Well,' she said, 'If that's how you feel, you'd better find a job.'

Part Two

What happened next –
In My Fashion

V
THE UNDERWEAR FACTORY

My first job was at an underwear factory. After climbing the grey stone stairs there was a huge clock-face with about two hundred numbers round its rim. After selecting my card from the rack on the wall I had to turn the arm of the clock till it reached my number and then punch in the time of arrival. Clocking in for somebody else meant getting the sack on the spot.

We all had to get clocked on by 8 am. Right on the dot of 8 o'clock the doors were locked and not opened again till 8.15. Anyone who arrived later than 8.15 had to go in, shame-faced, by the front door, at 8.30.

This lockout system was to make workers prompt, which it probably did, but meant lost wages and a fifteen-minute wait in the cold if the tram happened to be late. I could never see the point of a lockout system – if workers were needed why keep them outside?

At that time, in 1948, jobs were advertised in the *Leicester Mercury* in two or three long columns under 'Hosiery Operatives' and sub-headed 'Cutters', 'Menders', 'Overlockers' and other operations. Some said 'School Leavers Welcome'. The economy was booming and there were lots of jobs.

'School leavers' then meant fourteen-year-olds and that's how old I was when I first encountered the factory of Arthur Foister's Cherub works on Charles Street on a sunny September morning wearing a new dirndl skirt and carrying a school report. I walked in through the front entrance, the only time I would ever see it except when I was late. Standing in the oak panelled vestibule I pressed a bell that said, 'Please ring for attention'. A hatch opened like a speakeasy and a girl not much older than me said in a superior way, 'Wait here for the forelady.'

The forelady wore a white overall and I followed her to a small room and stood while she sat making notes at a desk. She took down my age, name and address and asked questions.

Forelady: 'Have you ever used a sewing machine?'

Me: 'Yes, I make my own clothes.'

Forelady: 'Did you make that skirt?'

Me: 'No, I bought it specially… '

Forelady: 'Well, specially for what?'

Me: 'For this interview.'

Forelady: 'When you make your own clothes do you cut them out yourself?'

Me: 'Yes.'

Forelady: 'Start on Monday, back entrance. The normal time is eight o'clock but, on your first day only, you start at nine. Ask for Mrs Wells in the cutting room on the top floor. The rate is twenty-five shillings weekly and you will be paid a week in hand.'

She didn't ask to see my school report but I was glad to get out into the street because my new skirt was too loose and needed hitching up.

Me: 'What does a week in hand mean?'

Mother: 'It means there's no pay the first week. You will be paid at the end of the second week for the work you did on the first.'

Me: 'But when do I get the second week's money?'

Mother : 'Not till you leave.'

It was all very hard to understand.

When I got to work all I could see was a huge room with wooden tables the length of the room. The people, at first glance, all looked the same. About fifty women and girls were facing each other as they walked up and down the benches cutting white cloth.

I stood in the doorway wearing a raincoat over a summer dress. I stood a long time. Nearby a woman was stretching so far over her counter that her feet were nearly off the ground. She saw me watching and, breathless, said, 'Are you waiting for Mrs Wells?'

I nodded.

'Nellie,' she shouted down the room, 'you're wanted.'

From far away I heard another voice shouting, 'Nellie, you're wanted.' After this came yet another shout, 'Tell her she's too early.'

The first woman relayed the answer to me, 'Nellie says you're too early. Wait a bit.'

When she appeared, Mrs Wells, an old woman of about forty-five in a pink overall, showed me the cloakroom.

Mrs Wells: 'Leave your coat here every day, outdoor clothes are not to be worn in the workroom. You can't smoke in here. There's the toilets and you can't smoke in there either.'

From fabric knitted on circular machines on the ground floor, the factory produced white cotton vests and pants for men and boys but first I had to learn how to use shears. Mrs Wells took me to a side-table where there were some lengths of cloth. After laying one layer on top of another she took a six-inch metal square and drew round it four times with blue chalk.

Mrs Wells: 'Watch how I cut these squares out, keep the shears flat, see, and keep the lines straight. Carry on cutting squares and I'll be back after break.'

I pulled up a stool.

Mrs Wells: 'What are you doing? You don't sit down to cut, you stand.'

I couldn't keep the fabric layers together at first and the shears were hurting my thumb. Then I spotted Thelma, who used to be at my school. She waved. It was wonderful to see somebody I knew. She came across.

Thelma: 'Why are you cutting already?'
Me: 'That's where they sent me.'
Thelma: 'Aren't you going to be a runabout then?'
Me: 'What's a runabout?'
Thelma: 'All new ones start as runabouts fetching and carrying from one floor to another.'
Me: 'What's the point of that?'
Thelma: 'They get to know the factory, they find out what they want to do. I've got to get back to my bench, see you at break.'
Me: 'What's the break?'
Thelma: 'You'll hear the trolley, we all queue up. You get a cup of tea and a sit down.'

After break Mrs Wells inspected my work, sniffing with disapproval at the crooked lines.

Mrs Wells: 'This looks as if it's been cut with a knife and fork. One cut with your shears, not three and don't make so much waste between the squares. Watch me carefully.'

Like lightning she marked up more squares slicing through the fabric so fast I could hardly see how she did it.

By the end of the week I was cutting circles and laying up five layers. Thelma showed me how to make myself a half-moon shaped leather apron to tie round my waist so I didn't wear my dress out when it rubbed on the bench.

Finally Mrs Wells began to show me how to cut vests and pants like a proper cutter. First I had to pull fabric from a roll and billow it in the air like waves before laying it along the bench loosely to relax the fabric while I examined it for flaws.

Mrs Wells: 'Everything you cut must be perfect, bad machining can be put right but if anything is cut wrong it's ruined, so cutting is very important.'

The cloth smelt oily and sometimes a seed of cotton was caught in the fibre making an uneven bump. I had to mark these faults.

After examining the fabric I pushed it back to one side ready to lay the first layer along the bench. Three or four more layers were spread over it with all edges precisely level and all the time keeping note of the position of flaws.

Then I laid the metal pattern on with its cut-out shape of necklines and armholes and drew round it with a triangle of chalk; I'd seen the girls sharpening chalk with the edge of their shears. I had to cut by pressing on the top of the shears as they scrunched through the layers. It was hard at first but Mrs Wells showed me how to wrap strips of cloth round the handles for comfort. Then the work was tied up in bundles of one dozen and I had to sign the ticket where it said 'Cutter'.

Eventually, when I was fast enough, I went on piecework and was paid, not by the week, but by the number of garments produced. Although office work was considered ladylike and superior, factory pay was much better, and piecework was best of all.

Older worker: 'The women here don't dress up. They don't put money on their backs but they've all got lovely homes.'

Some work paid better than others, little vests, for example, paid the same as big ones but little vests were quicker to cut. Even in shops today men's large vests cost the same as small ones but use twice as much fabric.

If the fabric had too many faults the foreman was called over and he sometimes allowed extra time for that batch.

Cutting was always done standing up. Nobody can stand still all day but walking along the bench was not especially tiring.

Every Friday I took my shears home for extra sharpening. These shears were strictly for cutting cloth, and never paper, which blunted them, were guarded carefully, and no worker ever used anyone else's shears.

Friend: 'Why is your finger hard down one side?'
Me: 'That's where the shears rub against the skin.'
Friend: 'I wouldn't ever do any job that spoiled my fingers.'

At twelve o'clock it was home to dinner, on bikes, on foot or by bus. Dinner was a cooked meal, with my three brothers and Mam and Dad. One brother was at a nursery and the other two were serving apprenticeships in printing. Apprenticeships for boys, factories for girls. We listened to *Workers' Playtime* on the Light Programme. These were live outside broadcasts from various factories and featured music, a comedian and a soprano usually singing 'One Fine Day' from *Madame Butterfly*. The broadcasts ended with community singing, and I returned to work for at 1 p.m.

It was always called 'dinner'. Lunch was something in a paper bag in your pocket for tea break.

A girl named Betty lived far away in the country at Markfield on a duck farm and I asked how she got home every day.

Betty: 'I don't go home. I have my dinner at Sylvia's house.
        She lives on Uppingham Road so it's near.'
Me: 'What's it like there?'
Betty: 'Very posh. They have side plates and as soon as we
        get in we have a cup of tea. I pay of course, I pay once
        a week.'

Back at work after dinner girls would call to each other:
'What did you have today?'
'Liver and onions, how about you?'
'Toad in the hole and rhubarb roly-poly.'
'I love jam roly-poly, raspberry jam's my favourite.'

I thought it strange to talk about food in this way, in our house it was considered gluttonous to talk about food. It was easy to chat to each other as we worked because, apart from the scrunch of shears, the cutting area was quiet. Girls who had been to the pictures the previous night would relate, at length, the whole plot as they worked and it was impossible to keep track of the story.

'Then he said to her, then she said to the other man, then they went back to the forest and that first man was waiting with a gun and before that…'

Bosses were shadowy figures who appeared in the workroom when there were problems. The two sons were called Mr David and Mr Roger and their father was Arthur Foister. These bosses were the only people in the factory who wore suits, usually navy and pin-striped. Clothes worn in the factory were markers of status. Workers wore old clothes and office staff dressed nicely. If a girl appeared looking smart under her overall she was bombarded with comments.

'Going out straight from work?'

'Who is he then?'

'I bet you think you look nice in that.'

Wearing hair curlers all day under a scarf was another sign you were 'going out straight from work.'

Each afternoon at around three o'clock, everybody started singing. I never knew how it began, it just seemed to happen, and every day the songs were the same. Not pop songs, not pub songs but old ballads of the kind found in a poetry anthology under the heading *Traditional Anonymous*.

This piece began the singing:

Where have you been all day Henry, my son,
Where have you been all day my beloved one?
In the meadow, in the meadow.'
Make my bed there's a pain in my head
And I want to lie down and die.
What will you leave your mother Henry, my son
What will you leave your mother my beloved one?
Silks and satins, silks and satins.
Make my bed there's a pain in my head
And I want to lie down and die.
What will you leave your father Henry, my son,
What will you leave your father my beloved one?
A rope to hang him, a rope to hang him.
Make my bed there's a pain in my head
And I want to lie down and die.

There are others verses now forgotten and it occurs to me that this song may have been part of a tradition of women singing at work and could have been passed down through the generations. It may also, like many ballads, have chronicled an actual event.

Everybody sang except for one, a girl named Linda, a girl who considered herself above us. Nellie, as I now called Mrs Wells, told us Linda took private singing lessons.

Me: 'Linda never joins in the singing.'
Mother: 'Why not?'
Me: 'It will spoil her voice because she's a colly tora soprano.'
Mother: 'Gracie Fields was a coloratura, she used to sing in the factory, so why can't Linda?'

On your birthday you were supposed to provide iced buns for everybody, passing them round in a lid from a big cardboard box. For my birthday I took petite fours instead, reduced price, from a posh bakers; they were not pleased about that ('You're supposed to bring buns with lemon icing on them'). I thought the petit fours were much prettier than buns.

Friday was payday and late in the afternoon we gathered at the top of the room to wait for Mrs Jackson in her white overall.

She stood with a tray of small brown packets and when she called our name we stepped forward to collect our wages.

The Friday before the annual holiday we collected two week's wages. Whatever we earned the week before, up to Wednesday, was doubled by Foisters for holiday pay. All week we'd worked non-stop, with hardly a break, in order to boost our output and earn extra. The name for this was 'scratting.' Scratting was frowned on normally because it could undermine the rate for a job but everybody scratted at holiday time.

This wage packet with holiday pay gave me a tremendous feeling of excitement. This was the biggest amount of money I had ever held in my hand and all the things I wanted were suddenly in my grasp. It was a sense of power and freedom, of having money to splash out on anything. No windfall since, no legacy, no prize money, has ever made me feel as wealthy as the thrill of that bulging wage packet.

VI
Before Sex was Invented

At home, while my brother giggled over Goya nudes on the Spanish stamps in his collection, I read the *News of the World*, a newspaper devoured in our house every Sunday. This was real life. Especially instructive were breach of promise cases where a woman, under promise of marriage 'anticipated the wedding night,' and the man was in court for failing to keep his promise to marry her.

The judge usually awarded money to the woman, especially, but not necessarily, if there was a baby involved. This breach of promise law, which was repealed soon afterwards, was puzzling. What would have happened if the man in court had said to the judge, 'All right, I don't want to, but I'll marry her.'

The talk of the cutting room was a girl named Julie who was engaged to be married.

Me: 'Julie Watson's brought her wedding forward to July instead of October.'

Mother: 'Oh yes… '

Me: 'And it's going to be in the registry office.'

Mother: 'She's having a baby.'

Me: 'Oh no. The church was fully booked.'

Mother: 'She's having baby you'll see. And when it's born she'll say it's premature. When you get married it'll be in a church and I want you to wear a white dress. You know what I mean.'

The talk of the whole factory was a new worker named Mandy in the mending section. Word went round that she told everybody she'd been to bed with her boyfriend. Going to bed with a boyfriend was shameful enough but talking about it openly was unheard of. One by one we left our benches and wandered into the mending section on pretend business to look at her.

Me: 'She looks quite normal.'
Jean: 'Common. Too much lipstick.'

Two days later she was sacked, ostensibly for bad work but it was really for something else.
   'Did she swear?'
   'No.'
   'What was it then?'
   'I'm not repeating it.'
   'Go on, tell us. What did she say?'
   'Ask Doris, she'll tell you.'

Doris wouldn't say but Margaret agreed to whisper it at the tea break and afterwards we returned to our benches shocked into silence.
   Mandy, apparently, while all the menders were open-mouthed, had regaled them with events of the previous Sunday afternoon with her boyfriend. This is what Mandy had said:
   'As I lay on the bed he threw a glass of cold water over me and said, 'That should cool you down.'

Sheila, the girl facing me along the bench had red hair that hung in waves down to her waist. She was tall, graceful and didn't know she was beautiful.

Sheila: 'I don't want anything to do with boys, they're awful. All they want to know is whether I've got red hair down there.'

Glancing up from her work, she said:
  'By the way, in case you're wondering, the answer's 'Yes'.'

Ann, nicely spoken and shy, had been married at sixteen to a Polish pilot named Yan, spelt with a J, and one year later he'd been killed in a training exercise.

Marion: 'Imagine being married to a man named Yan spelt with a J. That's really romantic.'
Me: 'And to be killed a year later, that's even more romantic.'
Marion: 'Shall we ask her about it?'
Me: 'About what?'
Marion: 'You know, the wedding night, what it was like.'
Me: 'You ask her. Go on, now, while she's sitting down.'
Jean: 'Marion's asking her. She's cheeky.'

We could see the two of them together at the far bench and we gathered round waiting for Marion's report. We knew what to do but not what it was like to do it. And here was somebody our age who could tell us.

Me: 'She's been gone a long time.'
Jean: 'Ann won't tell her anything.'
Me: 'Shhh… Here she comes. What did Ann say?'
Marion: 'Don't ask personal questions,' that's what she said.'
Jean: 'Told you.'
Marion: 'That's what she said first then she whispered something.'
Me: 'What did she whisper?'

Marion:	'She said Yan was very gentle and very tender.'
Jean:	'Well, go on… '
Marion:	'That's all she said, honest, he was very gentle and very tender.'
Jean:	'That's real romance, that is.'

French letters were a mystery; I had never seen one. One girl had a brother in the Navy who said French letters were supplied free to all the sailors. This was hard to believe because nobody would talk about such things to a brother.

Jane:	'They sell French letters in Boots.'
Sheila:	'How do you know?'
Jane:	'It says 'Durex sold here'.'
Sheila:	'They're not on the counter are they?'
Jane:	'Course not. You have to ask for them. You have to say 'packet of three please.'
Joyce:	'You know Joan in the machine room?'
Me:	'What about her?'
Joyce:	'Her husband has to use a special one made of silk and he has to wash it out every time.'
Me:	'Why?'
Joyce:	'Because the doctor says she mustn't have any more children.'

On the first day back after her honeymoon, we stared at a cutter named Pat, looking for signs on her face. Pat's husband was an older man, short and serious and boring. Always in gauntlet gloves and motorbike gear, he had no interest in other girls and didn't even look at us. Pat had had TB and mother said TB made girls pretty.

Carefully avoiding the word 'honeymoon' I asked if she'd had a nice holiday.

Pat: 'Yes, thank you. The bike broke down on the way to Devon and we had to spend the first night at the side of the road on the grass verge.'

We looked round at each other, mouthing "Grass verge!"

Ruth: 'Did you have love?'
Pat: 'Oh yes, we had love.'

VII
GOING YOUTH-HOSTELLING

Mother: 'You're not going and that's the end of it. If you
           think I'm letting you get into cars with strange men
           you've got another think coming young lady.'

Me: 'Why not?'

Mother: 'Because I say so, that's why not.'

Me: 'Everybody does it.'

Mother: 'Not my daughter.'

Me: 'You let David go.'

Mother: 'That's different and you know it.'

Me: 'I never have adventure. Carole has adventures. She's
           in the Girls' Venture Scouts, she goes.'

Mother: 'I'm not standing here arguing, the beds need
           making.'

We were talking about youth hostelling. Youth hostels with their big triangular Youth Hostelling Association (YHA) signs were dotted all over the country. At least two were in Leicestershire, at Knossington and Copt Oak, but they were too near. Most hikers headed for the hills of Derbyshire and its eight hostels.

The idea behind youth hostelling was to encourage young workers to leave the city at weekends. The YHA provided cheap accommodation to those travelling 'under their own steam', which meant walking, cycling or hitch-hiking, where you stood by the side of a road and used your thumb to try to get a lift. Overnight beds in a dormitory cost one shilling and sixpence and you could cook your own food.

It sounded like a great way to meet boys.

My brother went to hostels with a knapsack packed with bacon in greaseproof paper and a tin of beans. With his friend he would start at Red Hill roundabout at Birstall ready to hike north.

Although this was a popular and exciting pastime, I was not interested until I saw a YHA badge on the green jumper of Carole, a girl at work I admired. Carole was different from other girls, she never gossiped or joined in the singing but I liked her because she seemed grown-up and independent. As well as the Girls Venture Scouts she looked after a Brownie pack. Her fair hair was worn, not in curls like the rest of us, but short and straight.

I took her home for tea, knowing she'd be a pushover and after she'd gone mother said, 'What a sensible girl, she looks wholesome and refined.'

Me: 'Well, can I go with her then?'
Mother: 'I'll talk to your Dad.'

With strict instructions never to get into a vehicle with more than one man in we set off on the last Saturday of the year to Ilam Hall in Derbyshire because they were having a folk dancing party for the New Year.

The route was in four stages. Stage one as far as Loughborough, then a long walk to Hathern Road to hitch a lift to Derby and then on to the youth hostel.

After Derby we had not had a lift for about an hour when it began to snow; there were no weather forecasts then. Heads down under our hoods we trudged on in a blizzard that felt like sharp needles hitting my face. It was getting dark and traffic was thinning out when, at last, a van pulled up.

In the front seat I could just make out two men and a dog.

Me (in panic): 'No, no, Carole, say "No", there're two of them.'

Carole: 'Come on, it's the only chance we'll get.'
Man in van: 'Where you making for?'
Carole: 'Ilam youth hostel.'
Man in van: 'Jump in the back then, we'll take you there.'

'No, no!' I urged, tugging Carole's coat as she made for the back of the van.
Carole (over the engine noise): 'These men are OK, get in.'

My hands were so cold I couldn't open the van door but it was opened from inside where there were two more men. 'Come in lads,' one of them said helping us up and shutting the door against the wind.

Man in back of van: 'Ee they're not lads, they're young ladies.'

The two men were on wooden benches and we sat opposite with a sack between us on the floor; in the folds of the sack were four dead rabbits. While I sat trembling, from the cold and from worry in case mother found out, Carole talked to the men about Leicester Tigers. I thought it was an army regiment. In fact it was the Leicester rugby team. The wind banged against the sides as the van made its way through the blizzard.

Youth hostels were originally huge private houses and the oak-panelled entrance hall was full of warmth and activity as we queued up to sign in at the warden's office. From somewhere came the smell of bacon frying and a great clatter of pans.

Carole: 'That'll be the members' kitchen where we cook dinner. We queue for frying pans, and we have to wash them for the next person before we eat so food's always cold.'

Boys were running up and down the noisy staircase with its big curved banister carrying boxes of games. Two boys were speaking French.

A list of rules on the wall said:

Indoor shoes to be worn at all times
No smoking
No dogs
No noise after 11 p.m.
Sunday 11 a.m. prayers in the reading room are voluntary
HOUSE DUTIES ARE COMPULSORY

I'd heard about house duties, how people had to do a cleaning job before they could leave in the mornings, jobs like washing floors and polishing the stairs and how everybody tried to get out of it.

The person who ran the youth hostel was called the warden. He was handing over sleeping bags, made of green cotton sheeting with envelope tops to cover pillows. Then it was our turn to sign in.

Warden: 'I hoped you've booked, we're full.'
Carole: 'We're wayfarers.'
Warden: 'I'm sorry. We're full up.'
Carole: 'Both dormitories?'
Warden: 'Both dormitories.'
Carole: 'Is the family room vacant?'
Warden: 'All full.'
Carole: 'But there are supposed to be beds kept for wayfarers.'
Warden: 'Wayfarers' beds went at 6 o'clock. It's New Year's Eve.'

Handing over a slip of paper he said, 'Here, Mrs Drayling, second cottage past the post office. She'll take you in. Come back for the party about nine thirty. Next please.'

Out we went into the cold and the snow, tired and hungry

Me: 'What if the cottage is full?'
Carole: 'We'll go back and sleep in the games room. He's not allowed to turn anybody away.'

Carole knew the rules.

That small bright room in the cottage was like heaven. A big fire, smelling of wood smoke and coal, blazed in a black cooking range under a mantelpiece weighed down with photographs, mostly soldiers. Mrs Grayling hung our wet scarves and gloves on a string over the fireplace.

Mrs Grayling: 'Now what do you pay at the hostel?'
Carole: 'One and sixpence.'
Mrs Grayling: 'What about your supper?'
Carole: 'We've brought our own.'
Mrs Grayling: 'You can both sleep in this room, one on the sofa and one on the floor and I'll give you breakfast. You pay me two shillings each. And you can listen to *In Town Tonight* with us.'

'Thank you very much', I said quickly, dreading the very idea, 'but we're going to go to a folk dancing party at the hostel.'

'Oh,' said Mrs Grayling, 'you'll have to be back before half-past eleven. That's when we go to bed, New Year or no New Year.'

The fireside chairs and the sofa were covered with blankets and cushions, all colours and all hand knitted. Every time Mr Grayling tried to speak his wife interrupted so he didn't say much. In front of the fire was a rug made from strips of waste material pegged into a canvas backing, again all colours, and that's where Carole and I sat frying our bacon and cooking our beans. There were two ginger cats that whacked each other all the time as they tried to pinch the bacon which we were eating from the pan.

When the wind blew outside the smoke flickered up the chimney. The room was so cosy with the crackle of the fire and the click of Mrs Grayling's knitting pins that I began to wish we weren't going out at all. I felt bad about it because Carole had arranged the weekend but plucking up courage I whispered to her, 'Do you mind if I don't come with you tonight?'

She said, 'I wasn't going back anyway. I don't care for the warden.'

While we listened to the Light Programme on the wireless Mrs Grayling brought in a tray with four glasses of parsnip wine and some slices of Bakewell pudding, a round cake with yellow paste in the middle. The wine didn't taste very nice but I drank it. Afterwards Mr Grayling banked up the fire with slack, put a plate outside with a piece of coal on it and some coins to bring luck in the New Year, then they went to bed.

A paraffin heater stood in a corner of the outside lavatory to stop the pipes from freezing up and squares of newspaper hung from a nail on the wall.

Snuggled under blankets, me on the sofa and Carole on the floor, we lay awake talking by the dwindling firelight and listening to the bells of Ilam church ringing in the New Year.

At about five in the morning, when I couldn't sleep - because the fire had gone out and I was cold, even if both cats were snuggling up to me - there came a scraping noise from the front of the house.

Carole was nowhere to be seen.

The snow had stopped when I pushed the curtain aside, Carole, fully dressed, was clearing a path with a spade. As I pushed it open the bottom frame of the window rested on top of a snowdrift.

Carole: 'Put some clothes on and fetch another spade from the shed.'

108

Me: 'Can't Mr Grayling do it?'
Carole: 'No, we need to set off early. Hurry up.'

With snow up to our knees and with church bells ringing, we cleared a path, piling up the light fluffy snow on either side.

Me: 'Why do we have to set off so early?'
Carole: 'Sunday is a bad day for lifts, no lorries and most of the cars have families in: they won't stop. In another hour the roads will be full of hikers from the hostel. We need to get going and make for the café at Ashbourne. People in the café might give us a lift to Derby.'

Carole knew everything.

'Happy New Year both of you.' Mr Grayling was watching us from the front door in a long tweed coat over pyjamas. 'Well, you are good girls. Fancy saving me all that work. We'll not take any money from you both. Your breakfast's ready.'

It was the most we'd heard him say.

We sat on stools at a table in the scullery next to a shallow brown sink eating porridge and Derbyshire oatcakes.

Mrs Grayling wore a brown felt hat with a feather but she didn't eat anything because she was off to communion and had to go on an empty stomach. When she'd gone Carole left two shillings on the mantelpiece and nodded to me to do the same.

We set off up a winding lane with little walls at the side partly hidden under snowdrifts. The world looked a different place from the night before because we were in the middle of a great silence of snow.

Spread out on all sides, near and in the distance, were white hills divided by winding stonewalls that looked as if somebody had drawn them.

Carole seemed to like walking on ahead and I didn't mind because I was thinking about the next day at work and how to describe the adventure to the girls, of course I wouldn't mention the men in the van in case it got back to mother.

The first lift was in the front of a truck with milk churns in the back driven by a man who said he'd got up every morning at half-past three for twenty-two years.

I can't remember any more about the journey home.

I loved that cottage. And the cats.

VIII
MARSHA

Marsha was a vivacious girl with flashing eyes, thick black hair and a mischievous expression. She was a fast and skilful worker earning top wages and friendly with Nellie, who was her mentor, if mentors exist in hosiery factories. Nellie knitted two jumpers for Marsha, both the same, one to wear and one in the wash. I thought it strange to have two jumpers the same colour.

Joyce, calling across the room: 'It's my wedding anniversary next week, three years.'

Marsha: 'Three years and no babies. I don't think your marriage has been consumed.'

Nellie: 'Marsha! That's not the word. It's not 'consumed', it's 'consominated'.'

Marsha lived in a little back-to-back house. I went there once, into the bright front room with embroidered cloths and china cups. There were nine children in the family and every child had their own household job; the three-year-old was standing on a stool washing spoons. Eventually the eldest boy went to grammar school and became the dean of a cathedral.

With her trim figure and lively personality Marsha was never short of boyfriends. There was a Thursday man who took her to the theatre once a week, a Sunday afternoon man at a church club and several others queuing up for dates.

Mr Jenkins, the foreman at work, was a staid man in a white coat, he gave out the work and checked time slips. He was not the type to flirt but from the way he lingered round her counter it was obvious he liked Marsha.

One day we heard him ask her in an innocent and matter-of-fact way, 'You know those black hairs on your leg, do they go all the way to the top?'

We looked round at each other, open-mouthed and wondering how Marsha would react. She laid down her cutting shears, marched round the counter and faced him squarely. Banging her fists onto her hips, she stood and glared at him with fury till he slunk away whimpering, 'I'm sorry, I'm sorry, I'm sorry.'

He was over forty; she was seventeen.

It was Marsha who ran the perm club for a local hairdresser. Every factory had, among its workforce, people who organised raffles, sweepstakes on horses and other enterprises.

The perm club had eleven members willing to pay one pound a week for twelve weeks towards a perm that cost eleven pounds. Each week a name was drawn from a hat to see whose turn it was to get that week's perm. Marsha's reward was a free perm at week twelve, which, of course, had been paid for by the other members.

IX
Mr Cattell

New jobs were easy to find and workers often went from one factory to another, taking their friends with them. They knew which companies paid bonuses, which gave turkeys away at Christmas and which ones organised the best seaside outings in summer.

Friends in the drama group I belonged to worked in offices. Typists and invoice clerks needed a certificate from a commercial college and my family could not afford it but I decided to try for some kind of general office work even if the pay was not as good as cutting.

Among the advertisements in the *Leicester Mercury* were two jobs I fancied, one for a dress designer, the other for an office assistant. I applied, in writing, for both and found myself in a dress factory being interviewed by Mr Cattell, who was thin, pale and over six feet tall.

He seemed to have trouble finding somewhere to arrange his long legs as he sat talking to me. All the time he was speaking, which he did beautifully, he stroked and twisted his long flying officer moustache. Even now, whenever I hear the word 'gentleman' I always think of Mr Cattell in his brown shoes and brown, three-piece pin-striped suit and the fruity woodland whiff of his pipe.

Behind the glass I could see, and hear and smell, the whole factory and all those girls sitting on stools crouched over machines.

Mr Cattell: 'What are your qualifications, Miss Rogers?'

Me: 'Qualifications?'
Mr Cattell: 'Yes, your design qualifications.'
Me: 'Oh, I'm not qualified but I can draw dresses.'
Mr Cattell: I'm sure you're very good at drawing. Now tell me
           about your experience of knitwear design.'
Me: Well, I thought I could learn it here.'
Mr Cattell: Miss Rogers, I'm afraid designers need art college
           qualifications or at least two years' experience with a
           high class firm.'

When I said I didn't know about that he said, 'I'm very sorry you have had a journey for nothing. Will you please allow me to reimburse your bus fares?'

Like I said, a gentleman.

The office job interview was a pushover so I gave a week's notice to the underwear factory and turned up the following Monday all dressed up in an office worker's outfit, tweed skirt and jacket, bought on hire purchase, and a white blouse.

They showed me how to operate a Gestetner duplicating machine, which involved fastening a stencil to a roller, pouring in methylated spirits and turning a handle. Interesting work, and fun for the first half hour, but there was a lot of day left after that and nobody spoke to me. I hadn't realised boredom could be so awful and so terrifying.

Next day came a letter from Mr Cattell asking me to call back to see him.

'I hope I have not brought you here on a fool's errand, Miss Rogers,' he said, offering me a chair. Having no idea what he meant I replied in a posh voice, 'Not at all, sir.'

'There's something about you, something about you that…'

I waited, but instead of finishing the sentence, he told me there was a vacancy for a petton grader. I tried to look intelligent although I'd never heard of such a job. 'Somebody to take a paper petton,' (Ah! He meant a pattern.) 'for a small size dress and re-cut it in larger sizes.' If I wanted it I could have that job and I would be trained. I didn't go back to the office job, ever. They still owe me a day's pay.

X
THE DRESS FACTORY

I. and L. Stevens occupied the ground floor of a two-storey building on Charles Street. The upper floor housed a cigar factory owned by the brother-in-law of Mr Cattell. I once peeked inside to see long benches covered in huge dry leaves and the atmosphere was cold and dead. The dress factory had about fifty workers and produced top quality dresses under various labels including Susan Small. These dresses were displayed in the windows of city centre shops at a price equivalent to three or four weeks' wages.

There was a cutting room, pressing room, machine room and packing room. Despite the name they were not rooms, merely different areas of the factory, which was all one floor and meant that my work area was much noisier than Arthur Foister's Cherub works. Along one side were big windows but lights still had to be on all day. The boss, Mr Cattell, had his office at one end of the factory divided from us by a glass screen.

On that first morning I watched, confused and anxious, as Helen, a cutter-grader, took me through a list of specifications for dress sizes. I knew this work was for me, though, having seen all the colourful dresses hanging near the machines in various stages of being made up. Helen, who was friendly and encouraging, introduced me to people I would be in contact with including the sample machinist and the forelady.

Long after other workers had come in I noticed three girls wafting importantly through the factory and disappearing into a glass partitioned room at the far end.

Me:	'Who are they?'
Helen:	'They are the designers.'
Me:	'Why do they come late?'
Helen:	'Oh, designers don't keep factory hours.'
Me:	'Do they stay in that room?'
Helen	'Oh, no, they'll be in and out checking work, and they'll be checking your patterns.'
Me:	'I like their clothes.'
Helen:	'They go to fashion shows.'
Me:	'Fashion shows?'
Helen:	'They're always going to London shows and once a year they go to Ascot races. Julie's just married an architect, he sometimes comes in.'
Me:	'Comes in the factory?'
Helen:	'Of course, and the boyfriends of the other two, both artists, they come in.'

The only men working in the factory, apart from the caretaker and mechanic, were the packers who folded finished garments into boxes and labelled them ready for the van, which came weekly to transport garments to London. Also on the van but travelling on a dress rail, were new designs to be approved by head office.

The mechanic looked after the machinery if it broke down and he was always busy. Lockstitch machines joined two seams together just like ordinary domestic sewing machines. Overlock machines joined two seams in a way that allowed the fabric to stretch, otherwise the stitching on knitted fabric would break when the garment was pulled on. Overlocking also trimmed off excess fabric as it sewed the seam. Quality knitted dresses had both lockstitch and overlocked seams.

Three reels of cotton were needed on an overlocker and three needles had to be threaded. As soon as the operative pressed the foot pedal the cottons came whizzing off the spindles making a dash for the needles. Almost every tee-shirt and sweater today is made on these machines, an amazing invention. Overlockers worked at great speed and earned more than other workers except cutters.

A pin tuck machine picked up a tiny ridge of fabric and sewed it through from side to side creating a raised pattern on a yoke. A hemmer made a stitch at the bottom of a garment that was loose enough not to show through on the outside. All this machinery had to be kept in good order and, as well as the factory mechanic, Mike Harper from the Singer Sewing Machine Company was often called in. A girl's wages depended on piecework (irrespective of age they were called 'girls') and if the machine broke down they were idle and lost money.

XI
THE DESIGN OFFICE

The best thing about 'petton' grading was the position of the worktable, just outside the design office, from where I could see and hear much of what went on. Sometimes in the mornings, before the designers arrived, I would go in and touch things especially the buttons.

These button samples were on showcards. There were buttons of all shapes, buttons of glass and pearl, buttons of leather and buttons as big as biscuits. There were lace collars to feel and rolls of linen to smell. Dressmakers' dummies were used for creating patterns by draping muslin straight on to a body and once, when a dress was half pinned onto a dummy, I added some extra gathers.

The glass partition separating the room from the factory was covered in full-page advertisements for day dresses and evening gowns, torn out from French magazines, and they were reflected in the huge wall mirror opposite. Each one of these black and white pictures was a work of the photographer's art and now regarded as classic images.

Models struck a superior pose, in the sculpted styling and sumptuous fabrics, over signatures of the great names of Paris fashion houses, Balanciaga, Chanel, Hermes and Schiaparelli. These pictures, from French *Vogue* and *L'Officiel,* the standard records of couture, were replaced from time to time with any new ones that caught the eye of I. and L. Stevens' designers.

From my worktable outside I could often hear the designers talking. Everything French was good: French singers, French cloth, French cheese.

Rachel King, the head designer and after Mr Cattell the most important person there at I. and L. Stevens in Leicester, had been to Mr Cattell's holiday house at somewhere called Le Lavendue in France.

The designers spoke of French films they'd seen at the Floral Hall, but only black and white and only with sub-titles. Coloured films were 'so vile' and dubbing was one of the many things they sneered at along with the *Daily Mirror*, tinned soup and people who said 'brassiere' instead of 'bra.'

They read books called *Brideshead Revisited* and *Vile Bodies* by Evelyn Waugh, who turned out to be a man, and writers called Dostoyevsky, Tolstoy, Proust and Zola. I borrowed these books from the library the minute they were mentioned. None of them were hard to read except Proust, I couldn't see anything in him. The woman at the library had trouble finding a book called *Mennertarms*; she said, 'Do you mean *Men at Arms*?'

One Monday morning they were full of talk about Diaghilev, whose ballet they'd been to see in London. That was the 'bees' knees'. Anything good was always 'the bees' knees'. There was a picture of a Russian ballerina on display among the fashion pictures on the wall. She was leaning against a door and wearing a frumpy sweater. Underneath it said 'even age and crumpled tights cannot spoil the poetry of her legs.'

Apart from the occasions when a pattern piece needed checking, these girls, with tape measures permanently dangling round their necks, hardly noticed me at my work-table. Rachel was of small stature with straw-coloured hair and boyish good looks. Her features were flattish but she was amazingly attractive with a haughty expression as she pressed her fingers onto the pattern paper to show me how to shape an armhole or a neckline. When she stood that close her perfume smelt expensive and luxurious. The clothes she wore were plain and classic and of a quality I had never seen in a shop. Black French sweater, thin silk Jaeger scarf, tweed A-line skirt that tilted from side to side as she walked, and kitten-heeled shoes. The bees' knees.

XII
SATURDAY NIGHTS

The purpose of work was to earn enough to go out dressed up on Saturdays. All week long we looked forward to Saturday nights and the possibility of some excitement.

Morning was spent in town at Brucciani's spacious cream and green café in Horsefair Street, queuing up to be served by Mr B himself. 'Hurry along please. No more than six at one table. Hurry along *please*.'

All the smart youth of Leicester met there to talk and smoke and flirt at the round tables that could easily take a dozen of us. The shining ones from the art college had their own tables and we tried not to let them see us looking in their direction but they were too involved with each other ever to glance at us. The minute our cups were empty Mr B would clear the tables so the trick was always to have some coffee left in the cup.

Saturday afternoons were for getting ready, perhaps making a dress or trying out new make-up and hairdos.

The Palais de Danse in Humberstone Gate was a wonderful dance hall with its two bands one above the other, a fountain in the middle of the floor, twirling mirror ball and a balcony where a boy might invite you for coffee. But you had to think hard before accepting because you could be stuck with him all evening, the evening that began in the ladies cloakroom changing outdoor footwear into gold or silver dance shoes brought from home in a brown paper bag. A good ten minutes in front of the mirror then downstairs to stand at the side trying not to look hopeful but longing to hear, 'Can I have this dance please?'

It was not polite to refuse except if they were old or smelling of garlic; some foreigners never stood a chance. To avoid an unwelcome partner you had to look away when you saw him coming, that always put them off. If you were left without a partner there were strategies for saving face. Animated chatting to a friend with back turned to the dance floor or enthusiastic waves to imaginary people up in the balcony.

The bandsmen were old but the beat was infectious. Foxtrots, quick steps, waltzes and ladies 'excuse-me' quick steps where you tapped a man on the shoulder and he had to relinquish his partner and dance with you. A good looker could find himself with many different partners in the ladies 'excuse-me'. Of course nobody said they worked in a factory. That would be unthinkable. If somebody asked where you worked you made something up, 'office work,' 'air hostess,' 'management trainee.' The word 'factory' was out.

Jiving was the rage and some were terrific at it, especially little men, who could dance leaning backwards almost parallel with the floor and with one arm waving for balance they swung their partner so high you glimpsed her knickers.

The floor cleared for a good jiving couple. Men wore long jackets called drapes and crepe-soled shoes nicknamed 'brothel creepers'. Girls wore full skirts with stiff petticoats, sometimes two or three together, and they were meant to show.

The art school crowd sometimes came to the Palais but much later in the evening and they hadn't spent all afternoon getting ready; they wore the same clothes they wore for work, but still looked terrific. One quick dance with each other and they disappeared, probably to some party in the country to discuss Proust.

If you struck lucky by the end of the evening you might have found somebody interesting and, 'Can I walk you home?' was the next stage. While we queued on the stairs to collect coats and shoes the boys stood outside waiting for us, nobody had a car then. Their reward for walking us home was a quick kiss at the front gate where my Dad always happened to be putting out the milk bottles just as I arrived. After the kiss the invitation, 'Can I see you again?' We said 'Yes' and then didn't turn up if we weren't keen.

Sunday night under Kemps clock on the corner of Horsefair Street at seven o'clock was a typical meeting place. Of course the girl was never there first; we hid round the corner till we saw the boy, waited a few minutes, then ran up and apologised for being late. As my mother said, 'You must always let the boys think they are doing the chasing.'

The Odeon and the Savoy were popular cinemas for Sunday evening dates and the boy paid for the tickets. Girls offered to pay of course, in a half-hearted way, and sometimes bought the chocolates. On a Sunday in summer the meeting place might be St Margaret's Bus Station for the bus to Bradgate Park where boys hoping for a snog in the bracken carried a raincoat.

XIII
CHRISTMAS IN THE FACTORY

Christmas came early to the dress factory. From October onwards women put deposits on toys for their children; and deposits were lost if the rest of the money was not paid off within two months. These were expensive toys, bikes or pedal cars for boys, dolls and prams for girls. Some deposits were even put down on winter coats.

Me: 'Why do shops keep deposits and give you nothing?'
Dad: 'Workers are always robbed. Except in Russia.'

In mid-December a letterbox, fashioned from cardboard and red crepe paper, was placed in the middle of the factory and all our Christmas cards to each other were posted in it. Then came trimming up day when windows were criss-crossed with twisted bands of coloured paper and every dress rail and girder was festooned with lammetta, a type of tinsel. The dinner hour that day was bustling with activity; instead of going home we ate sandwiches.

Presents to each other were not surprises but the result of much excited bargaining over the weeks.

'You give me this, I'll give you that.'

'Here it is,' my friend announced, rushing in from the shops with a brown paper bag in her hand. Inside was something I'd looked forward to for weeks. A lipstick, not any lipstick, but a Max Factor lipstick. Max Factor, the makeup of the stars.

Although this was years after the war, luxury goods were only just coming in and there were queues at Lewis's department store when Max Factor consignments arrived. It was very expensive and special customers could reserve something.

'Only one item per customer please,' announced the Lewis's girls dolled up in white coats and plucked eyebrows, 'one lipstick or one refill but not both.'

And here was mine at last. To feel the weight of the gold case with its embossed pattern of tiny squares was to embrace that far off world of luxury and glamour beyond dreams.

To remove the top and twist the base till the shiny red cylinder emerged with a scent of sweet vanilla was to experience the world of open top cars with white steering wheels, driven by handsome men in white suits and shining partings leaning forward to light cigarettes for beautiful women with perfect hair and perfect teeth beneath skies that were ever blue. Coral Tone was the lipstick colour and just to say the name made me feel beautiful.

On the last afternoon before the three-day holiday, machines were switched off, two girls emptied the letterbox and delivered the cards round the room while trestle tables, covered in red crepe paper with scallops cut along the edge, displayed mince pies, sausage rolls and Walkers pork pies. Mr Cattell provided lemonade, beer and sherry. But not wine, wine was something only French people drank.

Afterwards, Mr Cattell passed cigars to the men and the place smelt lovely and Christmassy. While the office people stood at one end of the factory and the shining ones at the other, Mrs Bennett with her white thin face stood near the ironing boards and sang in a high-pitched voice.

'Trumpeter, what are you sounding now, is it the call I'm seeking?'

Then she sang some more verses, then something about treading light o'er the dead in the valley, then a few more verses. When she finished with, 'Till the trumpeter sounds the last rally,' a woman removed Mrs Bennett's glasses for her and wiped her eyes. I whispered to my friend, 'Why is she crying?'

'Because her son went down with the Ark Royal.'

'What's the Ark Royal?'

'Some ship.'

After tapping on a girder with a teaspoon Mr Cattell, with his beautiful upper class stammer, made a speech. First he thanked Mrs Bennett for her singing and said it was a fine thing to remember the boys who had given their lives for us in the war. Then he thanked all of us for our hard work in a difficult year, and asked us to convey his compliments of the season to our families and we could all go home an hour early. Somebody shouted, 'Three cheers for Mr Cattell,' and we did 'Hip-hip, hurray!'

After that everybody sang together, 'We wish you a Merry Christmas,' before hurrying out to join the crowds in Leicester market carrying last minute presents and buying turkeys.

XIV
THE DAFFODIL CARDIGAN

One afternoon I found, under the back of the counter behind a pipe, a dirty garment that had obviously been there for some time. Covered with dust, threads and fluff it appeared at first to be a greyish colour but the inside, unfolded was yellow and then I saw it. A blue label with the embroidered signature, 'Elsa Schiaparelli'. I had found a Paris couture cardigan.

From time to time head office in London purchased, at considerable cost, a couture garment from France with the sole purpose of sending it to Leicester to copy, not the design, but the underlying shape. Each manufacturer worked from their own basic pattern, known as 'the block' and from this block every pattern was developed. But because fashion silhouettes change in many subtle ways, the block needed regular updating with a new French pattern. The cardigan under my counter was one of these special purchases. It should have been sent back to London, but had been overlooked.

At first I kept it hidden but nobody came looking for it. In the end, I showed it to Mr Cattell and asked if I could borrow it for the weekend.

'What, this dirty thing?' he said, and I pointed to the Schiaparelli label.

'Ah, well, that's entirely a different matter,' he said, holding it out at arm's length and making sucking noises while he pondered.

Passing it back he whispered, 'Take it home and keep it,' adding, with a twinkle in his eye, 'best not to wear it for work.'

I loved Mr Cattell and wished he could be my father.

In the wash it came up a beautiful daffodil yellow. Knitted from mercerised cotton, a yarn that is twisted and polished after spinning to produce a sheen, the design was so simple that in the street nobody would have looked at it twice, but it was a perfect classic, short sleeved, summer cardigan. There were no seams anywhere because the welt, sleeves and stole were knitted into the shape. Nine mother-of-pearl buttons with rubber shanks for comfort formed the front fastening with hand-made buttonholes for strength.

The fit was superb, sitting so lightly on the waist and shoulders you hardly knew you were wearing it at all. Like all quality garments it bestowed elegance and poise on the wearer. Such is the effect of couture.

Every autumn the cardigan was put away in tissue paper till summer came round again and by the time it showed any sign of wear I had grown-up children. Such is the economic value of couture.

XV
MY BIG BREAK

I had been grading patterns into different sizes for about two months when, one Friday morning, Mr Cattell, on his way round the factory, asked how I was getting on. He wanted to know if the work was interesting and if there was enough space. I told him I liked the job but some of the designs were too plain at the back. He stopped and asked what I meant.

'This one, for example,' I explained, pointing to a blue woollen dress on its hanger.

Mr Cattell: 'What's wrong with it?'
Me: 'The back bodice has no feature.'
Mr Cattell: 'Does that matter?'
Me: 'It does if the fabric is plain.'
Mr Cattell: 'A woman can't see the back of a dress in a shop window.'
Me: 'She can when she tries it on.'
Mr Cattell: 'Really?'
Me: 'Yes, we twist round.'
Mr Cattell: 'Come with me to see Miss King.'

It was nearly dinnertime when the two of us stepped into the design office where the designers were putting coats on and preparing to leave.

'Do excuse us butting in Miss King, but Mary would like to try her hand at a design.'

Rachel, picking up her handbag, said in a dismissive manner, 'Oh anyone can design, can she cut a pattern?'

I felt silly because I couldn't; making an original pattern was a special skill.

'Of course she can't,' Mr Cattell answered in his polite way, 'but I'm sure you will help her with it,' and out the three of them went.

'Choose a fabric this afternoon,' he said, with an encouraging tap on my shoulder, 'and see what you can do.' Then he left the room as well.

I was alone, feeling foolish and wishing I'd not said a word about the designs.

Instead of going home I went to Woolworths and bought a writing pad without lines and a yellow pencil with a rubber at the end.

Fabrics were stored in the factory basement, a place that in summer was always cold and in winter smelt of fumes from the boiler. As soon as the afternoon shift began I went down to look through the new rolls of cloth with their swinging tickets and names of local firms such as Shipley Jayes and Jerseycraft.

These fabrics, with their comforting smell of new wool, were knitted on machines made in Leicester by companies like Mellor Bromley, Stibbe and Wildt. Local dye works coloured the yarns that had been spun nearby. Some of the wool would probably have come from a breed of sheep called Border Leicesters that grazed the wet green pastures of the eastern county. Leicestershire grass is so rich that farmers in the north of England used to rent the fields for grazing their stock.

I chose a honey-beige cloth and self-consciously walked through the factory behind the caretaker who carried the roll over his shoulder to my table. Sitting on a high stool I set about drawing collars and cuffs on the Woolworths pad, aware that other workers were watching. They were hard at work on machining, I was sketching.

After a while Rachel King came and stood looking over my shoulder, so close I could feel the fabric of her new skirt against my arm. Without saying a word and with a swish of her pleats she hurried away.

It was hard fighting the tears as I stared at my pathetic sketch, then came the slam of a magazine on the table. It was Rachel with French *Vogue* and a roll of paper.

'Put your drawings away,' she said, 'flick through this magazine very quickly. Then go through again page by page looking only at silhouettes and skirt length, nothing else. Spend at least an hour doing that. Then close it up and put it away. You will then be ready to draw. This is cartridge paper. Use it. If I can spare the time on Monday you can show me your ideas.'

In the history of the fashion industry few dresses could have had so much time spent on the first sketch. The weekend was given over to rubbing out and starting again; the whole family had a go at it.

On Monday, between two pieces of cardboard, I took the drawing to work. I worried because it was raining and I was afraid the cardboard would get wet. On top of it all the bus was held up because the conductor pressed the bell too soon and an old lady missed her footing as she stepped on. Buses did not have doors at that time. She had hurt her knee and I moved up to make room for her, immediately regretting it because the cardboard was a bit crushed.

All day I graded patterns and waited for a chance to show Rachel what I'd done, but there never seemed to be a suitable time to interrupt her comings and goings and by the middle of the afternoon I was desperate. I hadn't even dared to take a tea break in case I missed her. It was almost time to go home when I stood outside her door with French *Vogue* in one hand and the sketch in the other waiting for her to come out.

Me: 'Excuse me Rachel, I've finished with this magazine.'
Rachel: 'Put it in the office will you?'
Me: 'I wonder if you have time to look at my work?'

She looked surprised.

Rachel: 'Oh, I'd forgotten about that. You'd better bring it in.'

XVI
THAT FIRST PATTERN

Watching an expert at work, the speed, the precision, the balletic movements of the body, and the seemingly casual and effortless approach to a complicated task, is an exhilarating experience.

To make the pattern for my design, Rachel King began by pinning the sketch to the wall and sweeping the counter clear with a swish of her yardstick. Standing next to the roll of brown paper that stood in the corner like a tree trunk she uncoiled a section, slicing it free from the roll with a downward cut of her shears, a procedure requiring caution because paper can cut flesh deeper than a knife. After reverse rolling the paper to make it lie flat she spread it on the table, placing weights on the four corners. Next she lifted the block pattern from its wall hook and laid it on the paper, drawing round it and adding, with a flick of the ruler, front facings and seam allowances.

I stood watching her draw, freehand, the curve of an armhole, hardly daring to breath in the concentrated atmosphere of the situation and dreading anyone coming in to interrupt.

She glanced up at the sketch, 'Collar width?' she asked, tape measure at the ready and starting a quick fire dialogue.

Me: 'Four and a quarter inches.'
Rachel: 'Cuff width?'
Me: 'The same.'
Rachel: 'Why?'
Me: 'To match the collar.'

Rachel: 'Wrong. The eye deceives. For collar and cuff to look the same the cuffs must be cut narrower.'

Then she asked how deep I wanted the back bodice yoke.

Me: 'Five inches.'
Rachel: 'How will you get movement?'
Me: 'Centre box pleat.'
Rachel: 'Impossible. The seam will be too thick.'

Something inside sank. The back bodice was supposed to be cut like a man's shirt with a traditional pleat for movement and now she was saying it was not possible.

Me: 'But there must be movement, what can I do?'
Rachel: 'Ease it into the yoke. The machinist can push it under the machine foot, almost, but not quite, like gathering.'

I nodded, and along the seam she wrote 'ease', before writing instructions on all the other pattern pieces marking the grain of the fabric with an arrow, 'Cut to fold', 'Cut four', 'Cut linings extra'.

With the pencil lying almost horizontal to the paper she drew a curved side seam to the skirt and I wondered why it wasn't drawn straight with the yardstick. As if reading my mind, and without even glancing up, 'there are no straight lines on the human body.'

The pattern was now finished and on the front skirt Rachel wrote instructions for trimmings, 'Belt, buttons, tapes, linings.'

After swishing the waste paper off the table into the bin Rachel began to arrange the pieces to see how much fabric the dress would take, juggling big pieces this way and that, then fitting smaller pieces round them to make as little waste as possible.

'Let's call it one and three-quarter yards,' she said, writing it down. 'I'll leave you to draw a diagram of this layout. I'm away tomorrow, cut it out and if you make a mistake cut it again, never mind the cost, cost is irrelevant at this stage. Take it to my sample machinist and sit with her while she puts it together.'

Then she said something so amazing I thought I'd misheard.

'Be careful how you deal with her, a good machinist can make or mar your career.'

This woman, the city's top designer, whom I worshipped and feared, had spoken of my job as a career.

XVII
THEY LIKED THE DRESS

Workers in factories knew everything that was going on. Nobody told them anything and no meetings were called but nothing was secret for long. Even before they'd seen me sitting with Rachel's sample machinist they knew about my design as it progressed through the factory for lockstitching, contrast topstitching, overlocking, hemming, buttonholes and finishing. Some of the girls were resentful because workers do not push themselves forward, but others, especially older women, were interested and encouraging. A cutter, scuttling up to my table whispered, 'Can Mavis do your buttons?'

Me: 'No, no, Mavis is a presser.'
Cutter (with a wink): 'Mavis does them better.'
Me: 'OK. Ask Mavis to do them.'
Cutter: 'Oh, no, it's not my place to ask her. You've got to do it.'

Finally the dress was finished, looking good and hanging on the rail with other new designs. The honey beige garment was designed in a classic style, darted to the waist, long sleeves with cuffs and a straight skirt with a zipped side. The main feature was contrast topstitching round the cuffs and neckband in chocolate brown. This stitching was labour intensive requiring twenty rows one-eighth of an inch apart. What began as a sketch was now ready for wheeling out to the van bound for head office in London. A few days later factory gossip said Rachel and Mr Cattell were talking about me in his office. What could I have done wrong?

Before long Mr Cattell's secretary, an alarmingly efficient woman in grey, marched the length of the factory to stand behind me and announce in that superior tone unique to boss's secretaries, 'Mr Cattell would like to see you in his office.'

As usual the room smelt of pipe smoke. 'Come in, come in,' he said, indicating a seat near to Rachel. He was sitting in a leather swivel chair with a wooden rail round, his pipe resting on an ashtray next to a photo of his two boys outside their boarding school.

Picking up a paper from the desk he pushed backwards with his long legs; somebody said he used to be a Spitfire pilot but he would never have fitted into the cockpit.

'I'll come straight to the point, Mary, this memo has come from head office and I will read it to you, *We note that one of the new designs submitted is by a Miss Rogers. We do not know who Miss Rogers is but we are most impressed with the design.*' He waited for my reaction before saying, 'Now what do you think of that?'

I didn't know what I was supposed to say. These were the two top people in the factory. I was used to speaking to them but one at a time, not both together and now I was being asked for my opinion on something. 'Of course,' said Rachel, 'it's because it's new. Anything by a new designer always attracts.'

'Of course,' I said, ever eager to agree with her and grateful at least for something to say. Referring to her, as usual, in the third person, Mr Cattell said, 'What would you think about working as Miss King's assistant?'

'Assistant?' I muttered.

He explained that the job entailed helping her in any way that was required; Miss King would supervise my design work when she had time and he would arrange for me to spend one day a week at the art college. He added that there would be a small cut in my wages because he would need to engage a new pattern grader in my place.

'Your full title will be junior assistant designer.'

It was hard to take it in because all I wanted was to be alone and to repeat over and over in my head what the wonderful people at head office had said about my dress… *we are most impressed with the design.*

XVIII
MY NEW CAREER

Next morning a space was found for me in the design room and my new job began. This included nipping to the market to buy oranges for Rachel, watering Rachel's cyclamen and carrying things out to Rachel's car which stood on Charles Street; car parks were not invented then.

'I don't keep a dog and bark myself,' Rachel would joke from time to time adding that apprentices in Paris spend the first two years picking up pins from the floor.

Then there was the business of cups.

'Buy yourself a cup,' she said, 'then you can have tea with us instead of in the factory.'

In Woolworths I bought a beautiful cup and saucer in yellow. On one side of the cup was a relief of a thatched cottage with hollyhocks round the door. Unwrapping it in the office, I placed it proudly on the tea tray and the three of them burst into fits of laughter.

'It's hideous,' they shrieked while I stood there feeling small and silly. Their cups were by somebody called Suzie Cooper, blue with brown raised spots; I didn't know cups had to be designed. I couldn't understand why mine was hideous and discovered it was to do with something called good taste.

Mother: 'Never mind good taste, a cup with a cottage sticking out one side is good fun.'

Me: 'Rachel says good taste has to be acquired.'

Mother: 'Tell her some are born with it.'

There were other problems. For example, it was difficult to know what to do when visitors came. When Monsieur Berthiez came with his samples of French buttons the three girls gathered round but I carried on working. Sometimes Rachel would say, 'Do you want to come and look at these Mary?' and when that happened I never knew how long I was supposed to stand there.

Once when I spoke of 'my table' she said, 'This is not your table. You are working on a corner of mine.' Another time she took the hot spoon from her teacup and laid it on my bare arm; when I cried out with pain she laughed. Tearfully I told Gladys, one of the older women in the factory, what Rachel had done.

Gladys: 'She can be very spiteful.'
Me: 'But what shall I do?'
Gladys: 'Put up with it, learn what you can.'
Me: 'Why is she so horrible to me?'
Gladys: 'It's not just you. She's spoilt. She was an only child with no brothers and sisters to give her a good hiding when she needed one.'

The very idea of anyone giving Rachel a good hiding was impossible to imagine. I learned not to stand nearby when she stirred her tea and discovered that the other two designers also had to keep out of her way at teatime.

But this was a new and exciting world and I could borrow clothes for going out in the evenings. It was part of a designer's job to wear dresses from the sample rail in order to try them out. What happens to a neckline, for instance, when the wearer leans forward or twists round? Will the sleeve still feel comfortable with the natural movement of the arm and will the dress hang well after sitting in it for a few hours? Is there enough room in a pencil skirt for striding along the street or climbing stairs? Of course a borrowed garment had to be returned to the rail next morning ready for any machinist who needed to see how it was put together.

Another good thing was listening to Rachel talking to the three of us about fashion. She said there was a fashion in everything, the way you hold a cigarette, the names you give your children, the food you eat for breakfast. She said fashion was the 'living pulse of the world' and designers had to be aware of it by mixing with creative people and going to art shows.

Reading a good newspaper was essential because it shaped our taste. Going regularly to London was also important. Pointing to some pink fabric, she said, 'Money is irrelevant to good taste. Pink always looks cheap. That cinnamon colour there always looks expensive. They cost the same. Train your eye.'

XIX
LONDON

Soon the chance came to go to London.

There were only half-a-dozen people on the cold bus at six o'clock that dark November morning and they were different from the people on my usual bus. One of them was a coal miner with a lamp on his helmet and when he got off he smiled at everybody, including me. How could somebody smile with such an awful job? The other passengers would be regulars who knew each other and I must have looked strange all dressed up at that time of the morning in a gold duster coat and black velvet hat.

I was off to head office in London with Rachel and a designer named Teresa; my job was to carry a parcel of dresses and Teresa was going to meet the London staff. Rachel greeted me, shouting above the scream of an engine, 'That's a ridiculous colour for a train journey.'

Strolling backwards and forwards on the grimy platform at Leicester station, where the buffet windows still showed signs of wartime sticky tape, there were people in the trade nodding to each other; men with briefcases and boxes of samples.

Rachel chatted with another designer; they always stood out. Further along the platform was the usual sailor and, nearby, two of my brother's friends in National Service uniform smoking on a bench. But I pretended I didn't know them. Across the line was the Skegness platform where, in summer, queues of excited families struggled with enormous suitcases, quite different from today's London crowd.

Teresa, who was supposed to meet us at the station, had not turned up and I was alarmed to be told she wasn't coming; that meant I'd be alone all day with Rachel. What would I talk about? What could I say that would not feel silly?

There was the smell of soot and I was worried in case engine dirt was spoiling my coat, and my new suede court shoes were starting to pinch.

But this was like being on holiday and it seemed unreal to be sitting in a compartment for eight rattling along to London, watching fields whizzing by in the gathering light, while my friends were in the factory working. And it was paid for, and Mr Cattell, with his usual kindness, had taken me on one side and given me the money in advance.

For your throat's sake smoke Craven A, Maxwell House coffee - worth waiting for announced the makeshift hoardings hiding bomb sites as we approached St Pancras station where taxis were lined up on the platforms.

One taxi driver helped a businessman off the train and carried his briefcase for him.

Leicester Square, Marble Arch, Piccadilly, Covent Garden. Reading these famous names on the Underground wall was like being in the middle of the world but Rachel didn't even have to stop to read the way. With a rumbling swoosh trains burst from the tunnel and people entered them as casually as their own back doors to sit staring straight ahead looking bored. How could people be bored on the Underground train in London? I wondered.

The West End Headquarters of I. and L. Stevens had a boardroom for directors and a pink-carpeted showroom where I put down my parcel of dresses. When we entered the warm bustling machine room people greeted Rachel and I was amazed to hear the London accents. Just two hours away and people spoke differently.

Even before we took our coats off somebody said, 'Miss Draycott wants to see you immediately.'

Rachel looked worried. I followed her to a small workroom where a woman with her back to us was draping muslin. She wore a check wool dress, too long, with clumpy shoes. The model, a picture of boredom, was facing us and I had to look away because under the muslin her bare nipples could clearly be seen.

Without turning round and with no greeting, the older woman, waving an arm in the direction of a dress hanging on the wall opposite, said in a strange voice, 'Darts off centre, skirt off balance, see to it.' Taking the model by the arm she left the room and it was then I saw her dreadful face and was shocked. One side was stretched and twisted making one eye lower than the other and the mouth was pulled to one side, which would have accounted for the strange voice.

Taking her coat off Rachel examined the dress.

Rachel: 'Another Teresa disaster.'
Me: 'What's wrong?'
Rachel: 'A major pattern error.'
Me: 'It's not your fault. It's a mistake.'
Rachel: 'A designer is paid not to make mistakes. And in any case I am responsible for all the Leicester styling. Pass me those scissors.'

Unpicking is a laborious task where every stitch is removed carefully until the pieces separate. But Rachel snipped through the first stitch, put down the scissors, grabbed the two sides of the skirt and ripped the expensive material apart in one movement with a loud crack. Turning to me she said, 'Don't ever let me see you do that. Follow me, we deserve coffee.'

Over coffee Rachel explained that Miss Draycott had been injured as a child in a fire. She was a Paris-trained *directrice*, and everybody was afraid of her, including the bosses, but she ran the firm with an iron hand. I kept thinking about the model.

Me: 'I don't think the model was wearing anything under the muslin.'

Rachel: 'She was wearing talcum powder.'

It was the first time Rachel had ever joked with me and I was pleased.

Carrying on a conversation as we hurried along Oxford Street was difficult, not only was it hard to speak over the traffic noise, but it seemed that each time I admired some fashion in a window, Rachel was likely to say, 'it's awful'.

Some windows displayed a photograph of the new young queen who was to be crowned in a few months' time. My feet were hurting but it was exciting to be among so many people in their best clothes and makeup hurrying along on a working day. People were actually wearing the sort of outfits that were normally only seen in magazines.

Bourne and Hollingsworth's department store was heaps better than any Leicester shop and I would have liked to wander on my own but Rachel was heading for Liberty's in Regent Street where she had a friend. A man wearing a top hat and a green uniform greeted us at the entrance of the beautiful galleried building, which was more like a stately home than a shop.

Rachel introduced me to her friend as 'my assistant' and while they chatted on the scarf counter I was sent down to the basement to look at a fabric called 'cotton lawn', a cloth as crisp and delicate as the flowers printed on it yet it wore for years.

By the time I came back Rachel had bought three scarves. 'Pay more for a scarf than a dress', she said, 'because a scarf lasts a lifetime but a dress goes out of fashion. These are silk, a silk scarf holds colour and never fades.'

Once Rachel started talking fashion she couldn't stop and as I trailed after her round the store she was talking over her shoulder, 'Everything can be made a bit cheaper and a bit worse.'

'Wear the colour of your eyes in the daytime and the colour of your hair at night.'

'A black jumper always looks smart and with a different scarf and jewellery can look new every day.'

Back in the chilly darkness of Leicester as we climbed the station steps she said, 'You needn't rush to work in the morning, ten o'clock will do, and start sketching some of the London trends.'

When I confessed I hadn't been looking out for them she said, 'It's not what you see, it's what you absorb without knowing it, and next time you come to London don't wear new shoes.'

Out of the blue came a solicitor's letter asking me to be a witness for the lady who fell off the bus. I had no idea how she knew my name and address, but later I discovered that someone on the bus knew me and told the police what my name and address was. Mr Cattell gave me the day off and I wore a brown hat with a brim like witnesses wore in films.

Mother: 'On your way buy some daffodils for the lady and when you give them to her wish her all the best for the case.'

The woman and her husband were waiting for me with the solicitor who said I must not discuss my evidence.

Husband:'Oh, look she's brought us half a dozen daffs, that is kind.'

I was cross. It's funny how words can change something nice to something ordinary. 'Half a dozen daffs' made the spring flowers sound cheap. Afterwards a clerk asked what my daily wage was and when I said I was paid weekly he worked something out, passed me the money and gave me a paper to sign.

Dad: 'You can only accept money if you've lost wages, you silly girl.'
Me: 'What shall I do?'
Dad: 'You must give it Mr Cattell.'

Mr Cattell told me to keep it. Dad said if only all bosses were like that there would be no need for trade unions.

XX
ASCOT

Creative people need to move in creative circles and London designers were sent to Paris. Leicester staff went to London fashion shows and, once a year, in June, I. and L. Stevens sent its team to Ascot races.

With much excitement the three designers talked of little else except their Ascot outfits and I was, of course, extremely interested in their plans. A fitted coat of grey silk, cut from a Givenchy pattern, was being made in the workroom for Rachel. Linda said if you wore good shoes and carried a good bag the dress didn't matter at all. Teresa said she would borrow her aunt's crocodile bag but Teresa couldn't speak the truth by accident so nobody believed her. Long, thin umbrellas were the rage, more for posing than rain, and they were making umbrella covers to match their clothes. These were cut diagonally across the fabric like a man's tie; in fact, a man's tie was perfect for an umbrella cover once the narrow end was snipped off.

One afternoon while all this talk was going on, I was passing pins to Rachel who, perched on a stool, was draping a muslin bodice straight onto Gill, our thirty-four hip model. A model's job is to stand still and be stabbed with pins.

'What are you wearing for Ascot?' Rachel asked me, head on one side admiring her gathers.

I thought she was making fun of me in front of Gill and didn't reply. When she repeated the question I felt hurt and in my head was mother's voice, 'Our Mary, you let people walk all over you.' Holding the pin box steady I said timidly, 'You know I'm not going.'

She looked up, snatched a pin from between her teeth and snapped, 'I should jolly well hope you are going to Ascot, Mr Cattell has ordered four tickets for us.'

I was dumbstruck.

'Didn't you know?' she asked.

But I could not afford to go and would have to think of an excuse.

'Everything's paid for,' said Rachel, mind reading and talking to the muslin, 'entrance fees, dress allowance and out of pocket expenses.'

How I loved Mr Cattell.

Then something terrible happened and all the excitement of the Ascot trip evaporated.

Jim, the caretaker, a big man with a broom, gave me six shillings and the names of three horses on a slip of paper. Betting was illegal at the time except on a racecourse and I agreed to put the money on the first name. If it won, the winnings were to go on the second horse and, if that won, I was to put every penny on the third and final horse. Rachel was furious when she heard about it, 'We are not bookies' runners for caretakers.' I felt dreadful as if I was being ungrateful and letting her down.

Mother: 'You should have had more sense than to take his bet in the first place.'

Dad: 'Anyway, you're not old enough to bet on the tote, you have to be twenty-one.'

Mother: 'There's your excuse. Give him the money back and say you're too young.'

Me: 'No.'

Mother: 'Why ever not?'

Me: 'I promised, and the caretaker is nice to me, empties my basket first every morning.'

Dad:	'Well if that's how she feels Daisy, she'll have to do it. It's a free country.'
Mother:	'All right then but be discrete about it. When you get there make an excuse. Say you're going to find the Ladies then make your way to the Tote.'
Me:	'But I'll have to do that three times.'
Dad:	'No you won't. Just give the Tote the money and the horses' names, they'll see to it for you.'
Mam:	'Mind you keep the receipt.'
Dad:	'Well, that's all settled then.'
Me:	'What *is* the Tote?'

We set off early to Ascot on a sunny morning in Rachel's car with our hats in Marshall and Snelgrove hatboxes and a packed lunch.

Ascot race-goers traditionally picnic next to their cars on the grass before the first race at two o'clock. Everything was bright and colourful and the cut grass smelt wonderful.

Me:	'Why is everybody looking at us?'
Rachel:	'Not us. The car. They are looking at my car.'

The red MG was open-topped with running boards and chrome bumpers and it was so old the key had got lost and the ignition was turned with a nail file. Other cars were black and square and the one next to us had a chauffeur wearing leather gaiters.

I couldn't stop myself staring. From the boot, with help from another man, he unloaded a wicker hamper and opened it to reveal knives and forks strapped in rows under the lid. Then they unloaded five wooden dining chairs and a table. I whispered to Rachel, 'What sort of jobs would these people do?'

Rachel:	'Jobs? These people don't work.'

The men standing around the cars looked beautiful in their grey toppers and morning suits. They wore striped trousers and tailcoats with box pleats from the waist caught into grosgrain buttons. Tall men have a natural grace and they stood, holding white gloves behind their backs and balancing forward from the hips.

Using hatboxes as tables we ate our sandwiches and poured tea from flasks into china cups. Afterwards we took out the hats and spent ages putting them on. Rachel's was grey pleated silk to match her fitted coat and mine was a straw boater with daisies sewn round the crown to match the daisy in the lapel of my blue linen suit off the sample rail.

When we were ready to take photos somebody called, 'This way please, ladies,' and a man from the group next to us stood up and raised his glass of champagne.

Some people came by the special train from London that terminated in the Ascot grounds and we watched them parading down the grass track to the grandstand.

All the men were in grey and all the women were in a kind of uniform. This was either a dress and jacket or a suit of the colours found in liquorice allsorts, pinks, yellows and blues. To complete the outfits their shoes, bags and wide-brimmed hats were of the same colour and must have been specially dyed to match. Skirts were either pencil slim or ballerina length and full. I did not know such people existed, they looked so happy and confident and unhurried.

As they neared the grandstand the crowd parted and women bent at the knee to curtsey as Princess Margaret passed through with her chums.

Me: 'She's so petite and all that make-up.'
Rachel: 'That's for the newspaper photos.'
Me: 'She's the only one in a small hat.'

Rachel: 'That's because royalty has to be seen.'

Rachel had placed a bet on a French horse called Belle de Jour and to shrieks of excitement it came in first. While she'd gone to collect her winnings I pushed through the crowd to see Belle de Jour come stamping and snorting into the winner's enclosure surrounded by men in trilbies clapping. It was strange to see all the lovely clothes next to the farmyard smell of steaming horse manure. Belle de Jour was a chestnut horse but every inch of her coat looked black and shiny with sweat. Her eyes were glaring and I spoke to a man in a trilby.

Me: 'Is the horse ill?'
Man: 'Good God I hope not!'
Me: 'Why is she foaming at the mouth?'
Man: 'She's excited because she's won.'
Me: 'Does she know she's won?'
Man: 'They always know when they've won and they want to win again. If they lose a lot they get downhearted and have to be taken out for a few weeks.'

By the time we were back in Leicester it was late and we called at my house for a cup of coffee because the tyres were flat and Rachel had to pump them up.

I ran in first to warn mother and to ask her to change her slippers and use the best cups.

Afterwards mother, speaking of Rachel, said, 'I can't see anything in her, she's nothing special, she's just an ordinary girl.'

Mothers! What do they know?

Next morning I had to break the news to Big Jim that his first two horses won but it was all lost in the last race.

He carried on sweeping and didn't seem to mind at all. Dad said true gamblers expect to lose.

XXI
Fitting In

Adapting speech to fit in with people in the design office was easy because for a long time I had been making seismic shifts in vowels every night in a drama group called the Moat Players.

As well as accents there were differences in vocabulary. Instead of 'Mum and Dad' art college people said 'my parents,' a phrase not used by factory girls who went home to 'get something to eat' rather than 'a meal.'

I learnt to buy birthday cards without glitter; they had to be plain and definitely no poems. Another difference was in the matter of engagement rings. When girls in the factory became engaged their boyfriends saved up for months to buy the ring and everyone crowded round to admire it.

The traditional ring at that time was gold with platinum shoulders and two or three diamonds so small they were barely visible. If the engagement was subsequently broken off the girl would return the ring but the jeweller would not take it back at any price and the boy would be lucky to be offered a fraction of its value from a dealer. Like Dad said, 'workers are always robbed.'

But when Linda, a designer, and her architect boyfriend, became engaged, they chose a second-hand Victorian ring, with a garnet set in gold, paying far less than for a new ring and it would keep its value. The wedding was very different too.

Linda: 'On the invitation my father is inviting the guests directly to the reception in a hotel. We will join them there after the registry office.'

Me: 'You're being married in a registry office?'
Linda: 'Yes. Neither of us are churchgoers so it would be silly.'
Me: 'You know what the girls will think.'
Linda: 'They can think what they like.'

This disregard for the opinion of others showed an enviable independence of mind. Girls in the factory cared what others thought of them and did not want to appear different. Anyone who was in the Girl Guides for instance or went to an evening class was considered rather odd.

Linda invited me to her wedding reception and it was there I met Rachel's boyfriend, Martin. He was an artist, interested in stage design, and he wanted to know all about my drama group. Before long he joined and was building magnificent sets for us including one for *Brief Encounter* where the action took place in the buffet of a railway station.

In this way I was mixing with the art college crowd in the evenings as well as at work where we were making cotton dresses for summer. One of my favourites was a royal blue linen with white spots as big as old pennies. I. and L. Stevens advertised this dress in *Vogue* magazine. It had cap sleeves, an open neck with high collar, fitted darts to the waist and a calf length skirt cut from a complete circle of material with a hole in the centre for the waist. Although it took an extravagant amount of cloth, and the hems were always tricky, the result was a wonderful flared movement over the stiff petticoat.

In the full-page black and white picture the model, Fiona Campbell-Waters, with her short, dark hair, was photographed in profile on a high stool. With the dress, she wore a small white hat, white high-heeled sandals and white cotton gloves. Nobody was dressed properly that year without little gloves. The whole picture spoke of summer elegance and, of course, it went on the design room wall along with all the other magazine pages.

A new word was entering the fashion lexicon - 'Casuals'. The style originated with American college girls and meant, not dresses, but separates, a skirt and matching unstructured top. In the factory they were called jumper suits. Two-piece suits in a tailored style had always been popular but these casuals were simple pull-on tops and skirts. They were easy to wear and easy to make, which, as it turned out, was not good, either for our firm or for the British fashion industry as a whole. I. and L. Stevens never made trousers, this fashion was to come - and stay, a few years later.

XXII
NEW YORK

Sylvia: 'She's not coming, it's nearly ten.'

Jane: 'I've just seen her, she's here and she looks different.'

Sylvia: 'How d'ye mean?'

Jane: 'Her skin. It's sort of glowing.'

Mavis: 'Where is she now?'

Jane: 'Talking to Mr Cattell in his office, she'll be out soon.'

Mavis: 'Let's go and wait in the design office.'

Jane: 'I daren't do that.'

Sylvia: 'Yes we can, bring some work with you, think of something to ask her about it.'

Jane: 'It's all right for you, you're a sample hand – she'll tell us off.'

Sylvia: 'Come on, risk it.'

Cath: 'Can I come as well?'

The first day of January was a working day and the design office was crowded.

Rachel's parents were living in New York as they were doing business there. They sent for her to join them there for Christmas. On her return everybody wanted to know about New York.

Rachel wasn't pleased to see so many people in her room but she looked too tired to do anything about it. Her skin looked lovely. She took off her coat and showed off her American dress with its black velvet bolero edged with dangling lace bobbles. The girls gathered round to feel the fabric and between sips of coffee Rachel said, 'If you all knew what it was like none of you would stay here. Nobody sews and you can earn ten dollars just for turning a hem.'

Sylvia, the sample machinist asked the question that none of us dare ask.

'Your complexion looks nice, what is it?'

'Moisturiser,' said Rachel, 'they don't use sticky creams in the States. Water is what the skin needs.'

She told us about automat cafes where food was behind revolving glass and you put money in and took out any plate you fancied. She talked about something called 'pizza pie' and then she unwrapped a black beret with black sequins explaining that every major city has a rage and these berets were the rage of New York.

Me: 'What's it made from?'
Rachel: 'Angora.'
Me: 'Not the beret, this bag.'
Rachel: 'This is called polythene, everybody uses them, there
            are no paper bags there. See, it doesn't rip and it's
            waterproof.'

We passed it round to feel its softness and strength. This beautiful polythene bag was possibly the first one seen in the city.

Rachel: 'Never mind the bag. Do you want to know about
            the clothes or not?'

Finding a stool or leaning against the tables we were ready. 'Every dress in America is a step-in dress,' she explained, 'you can't sell a garment that has to be dragged over the head. In future we will do that here by using long back zips or front plackets.'

Next she unwrapped something like a small box camera, 'Press the button and look through,' she said to Jane. 'Now tell me what you can see.' Jane could not speak. 'Come along, pass it to Sylvia.' Sylvia was also speechless. Then it was my turn. The box was a viewer for slides and it took my breath away. A 3D photo of a park, blue sky, deep snow, people skiing and it looked so real in the bright sunshine that you were there, right there in the middle of it. Rachel's mother, in the foreground, wearing a red coat that contrasted with the white, looked so close you could have lifted her up with one finger.

By now more workers were trying to manoeuvre themselves inside and taking turns at the viewer when Mr Cattell came in and announced:

'This is all very exciting but please go back to work, ladies. Miss King is still recovering from her flight.'

As soon as they'd shuffled out he looked through the box and that night he took it home to show Mrs Cattell but not before it had been all round our factory and all round his brother-in-law's cigar factory upstairs.

XXIII
TERESA

When Teresa told me she was not an assistant designer but a senior designer I didn't believe her. Nobody believed Teresa. Her designs were not greatly original and her patterns were a joke. A piece that said, 'This side up' on the front also said 'This side up' on the back, and ninety dresses had been cut wrongly.

After that Rachel asked me to check all Teresa's patterns, which I was happy to do, even though it meant neglecting my own work. But when I discovered that she really was a senior designer and earning twice my salary all confidence in the value of my work evaporated. When something niggles every day it eats away at the pleasure of a job.

Mother: 'You should give your notice in and if they ask why you should tell them about Teresa.'

Me: 'I don't want to leave, I wouldn't be able to work anywhere else.'

Dad: 'Of course you can, you're as good as anybody.'

Me: 'I haven't got a diploma.'

Mother: 'Talent doesn't need a diploma, you'd soon get a better job. And nobody's appreciated in the place where they've learnt their trade.'

Dad: 'What does Teresa's father do?'

This was Dad's standard question for all my acquaintances and the one he judged people by.

Me: 'He owns a big firm, he makes fabrics.'

Dad: 'Oh, one of Mr Cattell's pals is he? That's how she got the job. They wouldn't allow that in Russia.'

In the end Mam said I should ask Mr Cattell for a rise. It was all very worrying but after two weeks I made an appointment with him and stood waiting at his door rehearsing my speech.

'Do sit down Mary,' he said, 'I think I know why you are here.'

I'd mentioned the appointment to Rachel because Dad told me it was wrong to go over anybody's head. She said, 'You must do what you want to do.'

Waiting till he'd shaken his Swan Vestas box to see if there were any matches left and then waiting till he'd filled his pipe from a tin of Three Nuns tobacco and set it alight, I began by saying how much I enjoyed the work and asking why my pay was a lot less than Teresa's. The room was soon full of the woody smoke that I liked.

After a few thoughtful puffs Mr Cattell said it would be improper to discuss the salary of anyone else and there were always anomalies in wages. Then the pipe went out and he lit it again and tidied his desk while I waited. He said he would change my title from assistant designer to designer and he would be pleased to give me a rise but it would not correspond to the wages of a college-trained person because there was always an extra emolument for a diploma.

As I was leaving he said, 'We wouldn't like to lose you, you know,' and I replied, 'Of course not, sir.'

I'm not sure what I expected from that interview but I came away feeling more miserable than when I went in.

XXIV
New Boyfriend

Not long after this, and overnight, the world became another place because I had a new boyfriend who knew about opera and wine. He was better looking than the art college boys and older, with a car, even if the roof leaked. Foreign, and therefore classless, Jewish, and therefore a citizen of the world.

We met at the Palais de Danse in Leicester, where, on Thursdays, there were evening dress dances sponsored by local manufacturers but open to the public. That night it was the annual Candy Ball for the confectionery industry and, wearing a black georgette three-quarter length dress, I went with my parents and brother.

A man asked me to dance, which was surprising, because I was talking to my brother at the time, but he looked nice, with dark hair, dark eyes and a friendly expression so I agreed. He said he was twenty-nine and from Czechoslovakia.

Everybody attending the ball had been given a box of confectionery. He wanted to know what was in my box and when I said 'Black Magic' he asked if I'd swap them for his liquorice allsorts. When I said they were hidden behind a curtain he said he'd done the same and could we make the change over after the dance. We danced again and then I took him to the balcony to meet my family.

When I introduced him to Mam and Dad he clicked his heels and made a little bow. I could tell by the way they glanced at each other that they were impressed.

Later, when mother stood up to look over the balcony he leapt to his feet.

'Oh,' said mother, 'are you leaving us?'

'Don't be silly, Daisy,' said Dad, 'he's not going anywhere. He's standing up because you are.'

In his car on the way home he made a confession.

'I'm not twenty-nine, I'm thirty and I'm not from Czechoslovakia, I'm from Germany.'

Next day my new dance partner called at the factory and I introduced him to Rachel. When he'd gone, I waited for the usual cynical comments she created for my boyfriends, creepy caterpillars and so forth. Instead she made an announcement to the design office:

'Did you notice how he put his jacket on, over the shoulders first, like a cape, that's the continental way. And did you see him click his heels?'

One night, Mother, who'd been waiting up for me watching the television, newly rented for the forthcoming coronation, was making me a cup of tea in the kitchen. I took my coat off slowly, hung it over the newel post at the bottom of the stairs and settled myself at the breakfast table before calling to her.

Me: 'I might marry this man.'
Mother (calling back): 'You are a funny thing. You've only
                known him three weeks.'
Me: 'Two.'
Mother (calling): 'D'ye want a biscuit?'
Me: 'He's coming tomorrow to ask you for my hand.'
Mother: 'Oh.'
Me: 'I mean it.'
Mother (dashing in from the kitchen with the tray): 'Oh, dear
                I'd better wake your Dad up.'

Me: 'And he's Jewish.'

Mother (putting the tray down): 'Oh! You can forget all about that, you silly girl. He won't marry you. They never marry out of their religion. And did you tell him we have no money?'

Now it was my turn to be engaged, and the girls crowded round to admire the Victorian ring with five amethysts from an antique shop in Stamford. When I told Rachel I was engaged she said, 'Well, as long as he's kind to you, that's what matters.' I thought this was a strange remark and still do. It was so unromantic. Rachel was now renting an Elizabethan vicarage and she seemed quite taken with my fiancé.

Rachel: 'Will you bring him if I invite you to a picnic in the grounds and does he eat Walkers pork sausages?'

Me: 'He *only* eats Walker's pork sausages.'

That summer the two of us were often invited out with Rachel's friends, usually to the stately homes that were newly open to the public. Everywhere else was closed on Sundays and trips to these country mansions with their architecture and paintings were extremely popular. Rachel laughed a lot with my fiancé and they made up silly jokes together in French.

   Although we were meeting socially I was still in awe of Rachel and conscious of the teacher-and-pupil basis of the friendship. After a lot of thought I decided to broach the subject of my wedding dress. What I really wanted was for her to design it and I chose an afternoon when Rachel was sitting with French Vogue and I was unpicking some pleats.

Me: 'What kind of wedding dress shall I choose?'

Rachel: 'What do you want?'

Me: 'Something that doesn't date.'

Rachel: 'All fashion will date.'

I said no more thinking the conversation was at an end but after a while she said, 'Follow the line of the body, that never changes.'

Me: 'What about material?'
Rachel: 'Which month?'
Me: 'July.'
Rachel: 'Cotton lace over cambric, three-quarter length skirt.'
Me (trying to sound casual) 'Is a high neck right for summer?'
Rachel: 'No, a round neck cut low with narrow shoulders and a high necked bolero of the same material. At least ten front buttons with shanks. And loop buttonholes. Pass me that pencil.'

The cotton lace dress was made in the factory two days later from material on Leicester market. The veil cut from a yard of tulle, was embroidered on the Cornelli machine. I think the whole lot cost two pounds ten shillings.

I thought Rachel was joking when she said her crowd had booked themselves into our honeymoon guesthouse in Cornwall, but it was true. Eight of us for breakfast every morning.

Back in Leicester, my new husband, calling in the factory one day, was surprised to be told I was out shopping for Rachel. That evening he said, 'My wife doesn't shop for anybody, ask Mr Cattell for a reference and get yourself a proper designer's job.'

Trembling and feeling like a traitor, I tapped on the door of Mr Cattell's office to ask him for a reference. He said, in his kindly way, 'do sit down, Mary.'

I explained why I had come to see him. I'd expected him to be surprised, but he didn't seem to be.

For a moment he was silent while he refilled and lit his pipe. Then he said, 'Mary, we will miss you but I am pleased you are seeking new pastures. Unfortunately, there are no vacancies here for a senior designer and I realise you need to further your career. You may give my name as a referee to your next employer. If they wish they may contact me.'

'Thank you,' I said, getting up to go.

He opened the door. 'Mary, your work here has been excellent. If your new position is not satisfactory, we would welcome you back.'

'Thank you,' I said.

Later, I wish I had thanked him more.

XXV
ENDPIECE

S.M. Hurst in Wigston doubled my salary when I went there to design mass-produced dresses for Marks and Spencer, their main customer. Regular inspections by an M & S team, who rolled down West Avenue in a chauffeured Daimler, checked there were no fewer than ten stitches to the inch and no deviation from the sample.

The designs weren't very exciting but I knew they had to look good on a hanger and have general appeal. They were high-quality affordable fashion.

A few years later I gave up dress design to be at home with my children. Most things in life happen by chance, and in 1964 I switched off the iron one afternoon to make a phone call.

I rang Marie Villiers, a friend from Leicester's Little Theatre, the local amateur theatre I belonged to. I asked Marie if I could watch her give a drama lesson. Marie was teaching drama two hours a week at South Fields College, now Leicester College.

'Oh, no dear,' she said, 'that's not possible, no teacher wants anyone watching.'

'Sorry. I wish I hadn't asked you.'

'No need to apologize, dear,' Marie said. 'It's funny you should ring because I'm thinking of giving it up. You would be just the person to take over.'

'I couldn't do that, I'm not qualified.'

'That doesn't matter dear, you've had lots of drama experience and they'd be interested in costume-making as well.'

'The thought of teaching terrifies me.'

'There's a teacher shortage, you could do it.'

So began twenty-five wonderful years as a full-time English and Drama lecturer in Further Education, among the exciting company of young people.

During that time, Prime Minister Harold Wilson, of blessed memory, created the Open University, where people like me who had missed out could take a degree in such life-enhancing subjects as literature, music and philosophy. The Open University completely changed my life.

One afternoon during a break in a garden bridge game, I was talking with three women friends, who were also retired, about our first jobs when one of them said, 'I never speak about my first job.'

Me: 'Why not?'
Anne (with a shudder): 'Oh, no, that's a part of my life that's long gone.'
Me: 'What did you do?'
Anne: 'If you must know I worked in a factory, making socks. There, I've said it!'
Me: 'What's wrong with that?'
Anne: 'Oh, you don't tell anybody you worked in a factory, it was a low job. My life's different now.'

The Leicester knitwear industry has all but vanished and I thought of the generations of skilled workers making dresses, jumpers, underwear and socks. How many like Anne, I wondered, were now ashamed of what they perceived as lowly work.

She was right, of course, factory work was for the poor and uneducated. Factory workers were considered 'common'. It made me think of all the beautiful girls who worked alongside me in a factory and the fun we had. And none of them were common.

Factories were not dark satanic mills, sewing needs daylight and factories had lots of windows. Leicester's vibrant and creative industry once helped to clothe the world with high-quality knitted outerwear and underwear. Today's school-leavers, filling Tesco's shelves, won't readily acquire the skills of making clothes and curtains for their families, nor any ability to recognise quality among the rails of charity shops.

Another city with a well known reputation for textiles was Chemnitz in Germany. Pre-war business contacts between the two cities provided life-saving connections for some refugees from Hitler's regime. Among them was the man I married who lost his family to Nazi gas chambers, an outrageous injustice which does not diminish.

With our two sons, we enjoyed fifty happy years together before his death in 2005.

Now I seem to have a new career as a writer. My first novel was published when I was 68 years old; nice things do happen to older people and I really like being old.

Marsha married a footballer. Rachel and her husband Martin visited America together and liked it so much they went to live there, in Connecticut. I still exchange Christmas cards with them.

THE END